Woodcarving

TECHNIQUES & PROJECTS

By James B. Johnstone and the Sunset Editorial Staff

Sunset Publishing Corporation • Menlo Park, California

_2946244_

Acknowledgments

We acknowledge with gratitude the aid of the many individuals who volunteered their carvings, time, and experience toward the preparation of this book. Special thanks are due to Alexander "Chips" Zeller, Mrs. Rosemary Nastich, and Marshall "Bud" Frack who contributed considerable time, effort, and many valuable suggestions.

The following corporations provided much additional information on maintenance and use of hand and power tools: Belsaw Machinery Co., Dal-Craft, Inc., Dremel Manufacturing Co., The Foredom Electric Company, McCulloch Corporation, Merit Abrasive Products Inc., Rockwell Manufacturing Company, and Wells Manufacturing Corporation.

No acknowledgment for a woodcarving book can be complete without recognition of the long term contributions of the members and officers of the National Wood Carvers Association and their excellent magazine *Chip Chats.* Information on membership, which includes the magazine, can be obtained through the Editor, Edward F. Gallenstein, 7424 Miami Avenue, Cincinnati, Ohio 45243, or the Secretary-Treasurer, Mrs. Catherine Flottemesch, 6871 Meadowdale Circle, Cincinnati, Ohio 45243. Many areas have local chapters holding regular meetings and shows.

Cover: Portuguese tray was carved using incised techniques (see instructions on page 46). Application of brown stain showed up need for additional touch-up carving. Carving by Alexander Zeller; photograph by George Selland, Moss Photography. Design consultant: John Flack.

Illustrations by Joseph Seney

Layout and Design: Lawrence A. Laukhuf

Editor, Sunset Books: Elizabeth L. Hogan

Eighteenth printing November 1992

Contents

An Introduction to Woodcarving

A

B

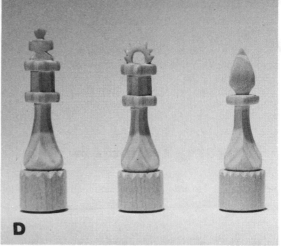

D

C

Tray shown in A and on front cover can be made following the instructions on page 46. Techniques for **B** are described on page 37, **C** on page 38, **D** on page 70, and **E** on pages 60 and 68.

Woodcarving offers the home craftsman a satisfying means of adding warmth and individuality to his surroundings. With a little practice, he can add beauty to utilitarian objects, produce decorative focal points for every day living, or create carved and sculptured art for the sheer joy of it.

There are hundreds of ordinary household items available at dime, hardware, and gift stores, that can be transformed into artistic treasures—personalized gems to be enjoyed in your own home or presented as gifts. House, room, and cupboard doors, drawers, shelf uprights and edges, door knobs and handles, banisters, frames, lintels, mantlepieces, screens, and headboards come quickly to mind. Serving trays and bowls, food preparation bowls and boards, and trivets can all be carved, and savored as ornaments between uses. Stark heavy pine furniture can be given an early mission, Mexican, or Spanish look with simple carving.

Each room or area in a room can be individualized with carved cupboard and door designs, medallions,

or handles. Or the scheme may be extended to an entire home. Carved gift items may be fancy with spur and stirrup designs or statuary horses for the equestrian, or simple, personalized abstract designs pleasing to the owner.

If, because of inexperience, you fear to cut into a door (or if it happens to be a hollow door), simply carve the pattern into a matching or contrasting wood, then apply the carving to the surface with wood or epoxy glue—or use screws. A fancier method is to cut into the door surface with a router or chisel and inlay the woodcarving.

Many cooks still like the old-fashioned wooden cooking spoons and paddles used by grandmother, but the only ones generally available today are dull, spindly sticks. A hand-carved cooking set of spoon, paddle, and spurtle with simple incised or low-relief carving on the handles makes a long-remembered gift. Houses of worship often need and would appreciate hand-carved items for use during services or for decoration in the sanctuaries. Schools and organizations value carved memorial and award plaques, furniture, and trophies. There are endless ways in which woodcarving can double the pleasures of life, both for you and for the recipients of your gifts.

WOODCARVING IN HISTORY

Wood has always held a special fascination for mankind. There are few art mediums in which the viewer's comments and interest are so often first concentrated on the material. The average person may not be able to tell the difference between cherry or mahogany, but he has an instinctive feeling of warmth for wood and a desire to touch it. Industry has long been able to manufacture plastic wood substitutes that provide hard, mar-resistant surfaces, but public acceptance has been slow for all but the most utilitarian furniture. The use of plastics on better quality

DISPLAY CASE has sides elaborately and intricately carved with symbols of sword and floral emblems.

least 2500 B.C. and is so lifelike that Arab workers who discovered it during an archeological dig named it after a look-alike local sheikh. In fact, it could just as easily represent anyone's neighbor striding along with a hiking staff in his hand.

Carvings in bone, ivory, horn, amber, and clay that predate surviving woodcarvings enable us to fill in many of the historical gaps, since similar methods of working were probably used. It is astonishing to look at some of these ancient pieces and recognize techniques still in use. The only real difference between Stone Age and modern carvers stems from the availability of up-to-date steel and power tools, but today's woodcarver can draw on the experience and genius of all of his predecessors for inspiration and guidance.

Most of us are familiar with the beauty of classic Greek sculpture. However, few are aware of the fact that many of the largest and best known sculptures of the time were in perishable wood. They were often painted or decorated with an inlay or overlay of precious metals and ivory. Travelers as late as the first and second centuries A.D. reported seeing the remnants of hundreds of wooden statues.

Religion, the sea, and furniture needs have conspired to keep woodcarving alive in the memory of man. Many, if not most, of the celebrated ancient and medieval woodcarvings were religiously inspired. Religious institutions employed woodcarvers, sculptors, and other artists at periods during the Dark Ages when there was otherwise little call for their work.

From the crudest hollow-log canoe through the majestic clipper ships, woodcarving and sculpting techniques have "gone down to the sea in ships." The oldest ship's figurehead still in existence is the vibrantly monstrous dragon's head of a Viking ship. Imperial Spain's magnificent galleons that carried home the plunder of the Americas were adorned with carving from bow to stern. There still are a few old-time figurehead carvers who survive by working for museums and parks, earning an occasional private commission decorating the stern transom of a pleasure boat.

Carved furniture is mentioned in the Old Testament, and in virtually every form of written record known. Except for fairly recent times in human history—such as the Puritan, Shaker, and the several war and post-war periods of austere styling—carving of some sort has been an integral part of all but the most inexpensive furniture. In fact, the custom furniture industry can be credited with preserving the nucleus of the woodcarver's art over the several long dry spells when woodcarving was considered passé or "merely artisan's work."

Michelangelo and Donatello carved many pieces in wood for churches and palaces in Italy. Grinling Gibbons (1648-1721), of English-Dutch extraction,

furniture has increased only in direct proportion to its partial success in achieving a closer approach in appearance and feel to real wood. Unless wood becomes so scarce and costly as to be driven completely off the furniture market, the substitutes will probably always play second fiddle simply because they lack the warmth of touch, the three-dimensional surface appearance of wood, and the ageless quality of growing old in beauty and grace as do wooden antiques.

In ancient history, a stick of wood probably shared honors with a lump of rock as man's first tool. Though wood lacked the durability of stone, its light weight and workability made it the material of choice for anything that had to be moved and handled.

Unfortunately, relatively few carved wooden artifacts have survived from mankind's early history simply because in most parts of the world, wood rots away in a generation or two. Oldest examples probably come from Egypt where the hot, dry air protected them from moisture-supported decay. The forty-three-inch-tall statue known as Sheikh-el-Beled, discovered at Karnak, Egypt, in 1860, dates from at

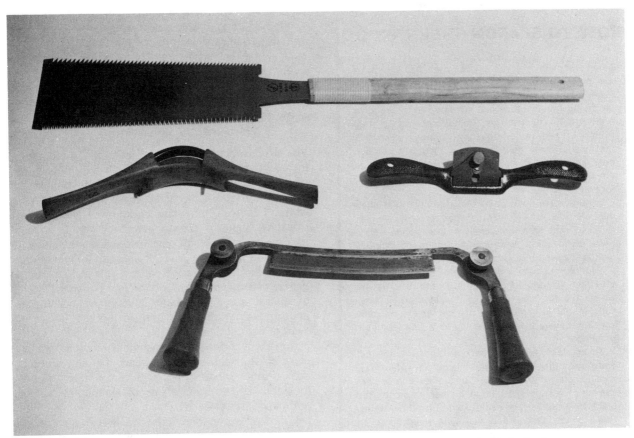

ANCIENT CUTTING TOOLS *still being used today by modern woodcarvers are the Japanese double-toothed saw (top), an inshave (left center), a spokeshave (right center), and a double-handled draw knife (bottom).*

produced a fantastic array of carvings for England's Charles II and George I, and executed innumerable private commissions, many for architect Sir Christopher Wren. His artistry with flowers, foliage, and fruit has probably never been equaled. Appointed Master Carver by George I, most of Gibbons' later works were carved to his designs by employees or apprentices—an early labor-saving practice common to many of the master artists.

Basic tools have changed surprisingly little since the time of the Pharaohs, when axes, awls, chisels, drills, knives, plum bobs, saws, and smoothing instruments similar to scrapers and planes were to be found in the tool boxes of the time. But somewhere in history, the East and West took different roads in the development of tools. In the Orient, planes and saws are designed to cut when pulled *toward* the user, while the Occident long ago opted in favor of saws and planes that cut when pushed *away* from the user. Remnants of pull type tools exist in the West as draw knives, spokeshaves, scrapers, and a few such related tools. As an experiment, try using a saw so that it cuts when pulled toward you (preferably a Japanese saw made for the purpose, though a light-weight Western saw or hacksaw blade will work) and the increased ease of control on fine work may well surprise you.

CHOOSING WOODS

Originally, carvers used the woods at hand, and it is probable that at some time virtually every wood has had some local use in carving. With the development of trade, rare and unique woods began to have wider distribution for use in the carving of religious and royal articles. But only in relatively recent times has a wide variety of exotic woods been readily available to the woodcarver. This freedom of selection, however, imposes the burden of having to choose wood with characteristics suitable to the particular project. For example, porous red oak makes an inferior wine cask, but white oak is excellent because its tyloses-plugged pores make it highly resistant to water.

In carving vessels intended to hold food, avoid woods that have a distinctive or resinous flavor or smell, or that leach color in contact with water, food acids, or alkalis. Ash, beech, black gum, cottonwood,

HOW TO SEASON GREEN WOOD

Membership in a coven of wood witches might be the best diploma for the wood seasoner. Science seems to have thrown up its hands on the subject of air-drying green woods and retreated to the relative predictability of kiln and radio-frequency drying. Both kiln and radio-frequency drying are beyond the means of the do-it-yourselfer, though if you live near such installations you may be able to persuade the operators to dry small batches of home-cut wood for you.

Air-drying, in spite of its unpredictability, is often the only hope for the average woodcarver who wants to carve rare or commercially scarce woods—such as diamond willow, madrone, manzanita, persimmon, ginkgo, baywood, or Osage orange.

Your worst enemy in air-drying or seasoning is the too-rapid evaporation of surface and end layers versus the too slow drying of the interior. This results in cracks, splits, and shakes which, in some species, can reduce a large log to a tiny, carvable remainder.

To dry logs, leave the bark on and coat the cut ends—including branch cut-off points—with wax, shellac, one of the commercial lumber end-sealers available through most large lumber yards, or the black tree-and-grafting sealer sold at most nurseries. Some of the dark sealers will stain wood up to an inch or so into the end grain, so allow for this when cutting logs to lengths for specific jobs.

Raise logs off the ground and separate from adjoining logs to allow air circulation. A shelter from rain, snow, and strong sun is helpful. A warm dry attic, basement, or shed is ideal. Keep watch on the ends and reseal if cracks appear in sealant. Control humidity with a plastic tarpaulin if drying appears too fast. Use PEG treatment for green logs.

Seasoning time varies according to the density of the wood, water content, cross-section thickness of the wood, temperature, and humidity. Only experience is a fairly accurate guide. Generally, relative weights of woods give a fair clue to seasoning time, within the scale of 1 through 4 summers. Some pines and firs dry reasonably well in one year as logs, and in one or two months as cut lumber (in a relatively dry summer). A red oak, manzanita, or rosewood may take several summers in the log form.

If you have the equipment, you might bore a hole through the center of the log heartwood, which will greatly speed drying. A variation on this was used by medieval carvers who often had to work with less-than-dry woods. They hollowed the backs of statues intended for wall-mounting, leaving a carved shell which dried with a minimum of cracking.

Drying your own wood will bring many a temporary heartache over a log split beyond use, but the odds are you will have enough successes with a few exotic logs to make up for all the failures.

cucumber, harewood, magnolia, myrtle (Oregon or California), sugar and soft maples, red gum, and yellow poplar are all good choices for containers such as bowls and plates. Cherry, birch, mahogany, Luan, several varieties of rosewood, and walnut are also often used for their inherent beauty. Be careful of the rosewoods (*Dalbergia* family) and their relatives where food may be involved—some members are allergenic, notably Cocobolo.

Visual characteristics of interest to the woodcarver include overall color, relative width and local color of spring and summer wood, and grain texture of the finished surface. Colors run from the almost dead white of English harewood through the typical hues of yellow poplar and greenheart; the infinite shades of brown, gray, black, and red of manzanita and padauk, to the true purple of amaranth. Figures and color patterns can vary from the almost featureless quality of basswood through the fine pin-stripe figure of quarter-sawn mahogany, the intricate flamboyance of walnut stump or burl; to the wide stripe or swirl of flat-cut fir or Scotch pine.

Surface textures of the finished woods run from the waxy smoothness of lignum vitae, the silky smoothness of ebony, basswood, and hard maple, through the increasingly open grains of mahogany, walnut, teak, ash, and oak.

With few exceptions, sapwood is lighter in shade and often a different color than its natural heartwood. Since heartwood is the most desirable portion of the tree, its color is considered representative of the wood. Walnut sapwood may be darkened to almost heartwood color by extended steam treating, and is often done commercially. Use of the contrasting colors of both sapwood and heartwood in a single carving calls for good judgment if the appearance of gimmickry is to be avoided, but can be very effective when well done.

Physical characteristics of special interest to the carver are: weight and hardness; nature of the grain (homogeneous or stringy, straight or curly, close or coarse); workability; and resistance to splitting under hand and power tools (see the chart on pages 10 and 11).

Weight and hardness are usually related, affect the amount of force necessary to carve, and roughly indicate the rate of penetration of chemicals such as PEG (see opposite page).

Grain character affects the ease of tool control while carving. Homogeneous, straight, close grains allow easy control. Stringy, curly, coarse grains present obstacles to good control.

Workability and resistance to splitting are related to hardness and grain, and are indications of the work required to obtain a good surface and of the ease with which material can be removed by gouging without splitting the piece.

"PEG" CAN STOP SPLITTING

Polyethylene Glycol 1000—commonly referred to as PEG—has been hailed as a miracle cure for checking, cracking, splitting, and all unwanted dimensional changes.

It is not a miracle cure-all. With understanding and correct use it can reduce or prevent these and other undesirable dimensional changes in *some* woods. But it does have side effects. It is hygroscopic (tending to absorb moisture) and unless sealed will become tacky and leak from the wood in humid weather or on contact with water. The only finishes that will dependably adhere to PEG-treated wood are some of the air-drying polyurethane varnishes, and these may or may not fit in with the carver's plans.

Wood density and porosity vary widely within a given species, to say nothing of the even greater differences between species. This makes it difficult to give hard-and-fast rules for PEG use. As an example, two sticks of apparently identical maple were experimentally PEG-treated in the same tank at the same time, yet responded in totally different ways. One remained check-free for two years, the other checked and warped within a week; both had been stored together under identical conditions.

You will find that density, porosity, and thickness of the wood, temperature and strength of PEG solution, and duration of treatment are all factors. Hint: wood-turners and carvers have found that rough-shaping to within a fraction of an inch of finished dimensions greatly reduces time of treatment, since little time is wasted treating wood that must be removed.

Here are some good starting points for experiments with PEG-treating (see below). The figures apply to *walnut*, in approximately the thickness given. (Thickness here refers to the smallest dimension of the largest section of a carving. Thus treatment time for a solid-cone shape would be dictated by the thickness through the large end; treatment time for a triangle cut from a ¾-inch board would be controlled by the ¾-inch dimension.)

30% solution at 70° F.

Time	Thickness
21 days	1½ inches
60 days	3 inches

50% solution at 70° F.

15 days	1½ inches
45 days	3 inches

30% solution at 140° F.

8 days	1½ inches
30 days	3 inches

50% solution at 140° F.

4 days	1½ inches
15 days	3 inches

The relative hardness rating of the woods in the chart on pages 10-11 can be used as a rough guide to time adjustments given in the next column.

Hardness	Time Adjustment
Soft	⅓ time given for walnut
Medium	½ time given for walnut
Medium-Hard	Same time as walnut
Hard	3 times given for walnut
Very Hard	5 times given for walnut and *up* usually with 140° F. or higher

Times given are for green wood or previously-dried wood that has been thoroughly water-soaked before PEG treatment. One to six weeks of soaking may be necessary, depending on porosity of the wood. The pre-soak is necessary for dry woods since PEG depends on water to provide a pathway for entry into the wood structure. Remember, the soaking and PEG treatment can rehabilitate *some* checked carvings.

Always use glass, ceramic, or plastic containers for PEG-treating. Avoid metals because some woods become stained when PEG-soaked in metal containers. A plastic garbage can, or a heavy plastic bag supported in a can or box, will work well for home use. Arrange a cover to reduce evaporation.

An immersion heater (in glass, plastic, or ceramic jacket) with a thermostat control is ideal, but one or more light bulbs suspended just above the liquid

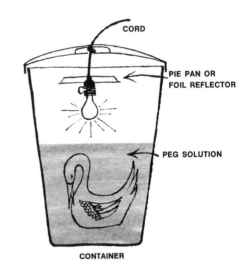

CORD

PIE PAN OR FOIL REFLECTOR

PEG SOLUTION

CONTAINER

surface work well. It is a good idea to provide aluminum foil reflectors to direct light and heat straight down into the water and *away* from the plastic container exposed above water level.

Examine container regularly for leaks and evaporation. Add water to maintain fluid level. If fungus or a scum forms, add 2% sodium pentachlorophenolate—a fungicide used in wood preservative products and available through some paint and hardware stores.

Wood Characteristics

	Pounds per cu. ft.	Approx. hardness	Grain	Color (heartwood)	Split resistance	Comments
Alder	28	Medium	Unobtrusive	Pale pink to brown	Good	Good to work with; easy to glue; can be finished to look like other woods.
Ash	42	Hard	Moderately open	Grey-white to brown with red tints	Good	Easy to work; can be bent to shape.
Aspen	26	Soft	Mild; close	White to light tan	Good	Works, glues, and finishes well. Checks.
Avodire	36	Medium hard	Mild; wavy	Creamy gold to white	Good	Moderately hard to carve, but finishes well.
Balsa	8	Extremely soft	Open	White to pale pinkish-white	Good	Spongy texture; needs razor sharp tools; damages easily.
Basswood	26	Soft	Unobtrusive; close	White through creamy brown	Good	Carves well; good for fine detail.
Beech	45	Hard	Moderate with conspicuous rays; close	White with reddish-brown tinge	High	Odorless and tasteless; excellent for carving utensils. Checks.
Birch	43	Hard	Moderate; close	Creamy to light reddish-brown	High	Works and burnishes well; hard to damage. Checks.
Boxwood		Extremely hard	Moderate; close	Creamy to yellow	High	Hard to carve; used mainly for wood engravings and chisel handles.
Butternut	27	Medium	Moderate	Creamy tan	Good	Carves easily, but chips readily.
Cedar, Red Eastern	29	Medium hard	Knotty; close; prominent	Pinkish reds with creamy streaks	Low	Easy to cut except for knots; is brittle; has odor and taste.
Western	24	Medium	Prominent; close	Pinkish-brown to dull-brown	Low	
Cherry, Black	35	Medium hard	Moderate; very close	Light to dark reddish-brown	High	Moderately hard to cut but finishes well.
Chestnut	30	Medium hard	Moderate; coarse; wormy	Greyish to reddish-brown	Good	Fairly easy to work; burnishes well. Checks easily.
Cottonwood	26	Medium	Unobtrusive; close	Grey-white to brown	Good	Works easily; good for fine detail.
Cypress	32	Medium hard	Prominently wide; close	Pale to black brown with red tinge	Low	Works easily. An excellent softwood for exterior use.
Ebony Gaboon	50	Extremely hard	Very indistinct; close	Black	High	
India	62	Extremely hard	Very indistinct; close	Black	High	Very brittle; hard to carve. Finishes well.
Macassar		Extremely hard	Very indistinct; close	Black with yellow-brown streaks	High	
Elm American	35	Medium hard	Moderate; very close	Light to dark; brown with reddish-brown streaks	High	
Rock	44	Hard	Moderate; very close	Brown to dark-brown with red tint	High	Moderately hard to work; bends, glues, and finishes well.
Eucalyptus (see Gum, Blue)						
Fir Douglas	33	Medium hard	Wide	Orange-red brown	Fair	Softwood. Wild grain slows carving. Has resin canals, leaks.
White	25	Medium	Wide	White to reddish-brown	Fair	Softwood; has no resin canals.
Gum Black (Tupelo)	36	Medium hard	Moderate	Brown	High	Works moderately well. Checks.
Blue (Eucalyptus)	50	Hard	Moderate; open	Creamy to pink with streaks	High	Hard but clean carving. Checks.
Sweet	34	Medium hard	Moderate; figure	Reddish-brown	High	Works and finishes well. Checks.
Hackberry	37	Medium hard	Distinct; coarse	Yellowish to greenish-grey	Low	Split prone; moderately hard to carve.
Hickory (average)	42-52	Hard	Moderate with visible pores	Brown to reddish-brown	Good	Hard to carve.
Holly	40	Medium hard	Virtually none; very close	White, but darkens to brown with age	High	Excellent for detail; moderately hard carving.
Lignum Vitae	80	Extremely hard	Moderate; very close	Olive to very dark-brown with light streaks	High	Very hard to carve, but takes a beautiful and natural burnish.
Madrone	45	Hard	Moderate, with pronounced rays; very close	Reddish-brown	Good	Hard to carve; has good color and grain.
Magnolia (Cucumber)	34	Medium hard	Indistinct; close	Pale green-brown heart with yellow sapwood	Good	Moderately good for carving. Glues and finishes well.

	Pounds per cu. ft.	Approx. hardness	Grain	Color (heartwood)	Split resistance	Comments
Mahogany						
African	31	Medium hard	Moderate to outstanding figure; open	Pinkish brown to tan brown	Good	Carves easily.
Cuban	40	Hard	Moderate, with out-standing figure; open	Yellow tan through gold-brown and brown-red	Good	Excellent to work with. Burnishes and finishes well.
Honduras	34	Medium hard	Moderate to outstanding figure; open	Yellow-brown through rich red	Good	Carves easily.
Philippine (See Philippine Hardwood)						
Maple	33-44	Medium hard to hard	Moderate with prominent rays; close	Creamy to light reddish-brown	High	Medium hard to carve.
Myrtle, California or Oregon	39	Hard	Moderate; close	Gold-brown with yellow or green cast	Good	Turns well; moderately hard to carve; finishes well.
Oak						
American Red	44	Hard	Pronounced pattern, rays, and pores; coarse	Grey-brown with red cast	Good	Good to work with.
American White	47	Hard	Pronounced pattern, rays, and pores; coarse	Light-grey to yellow-brown	Good	Easy to carve; not recommended for fine detail. Excellent for durability.
English Brown	45	Hard	Pronounced pattern, rays, and pores; coarse	Light-tan to dark-brown	Good	Excellent for carving.
Padauk, Andaman	45	Hard	Moderate; close	Gold-brown to violet red	High	Brittle; hard to carve.
Pecan	47	Hard	Distinct; open pores; close	Reddish-brown	Good	Good for carving.
Persimmon	52	Hard	Distinct; very close	Brown with stripes	High	Moderately hard to carve; finishes well.
Philippine Hardwoods misnamed "Mahoganies"						
Red Luan	36	Medium hard	Moderate, but coarse and stringy	Red to brown	Good	Best samples carve easily; end grain sometimes difficult to smooth. Avoid lighter straw-colored lumber; it tends to be stringier.
Tanguile	39	Medium hard	Moderate, but coarse and stringy	Dark to reddish-brown	Good	
Pine, White						
Northern	25	Soft	Indistinct; very close	Creamy-white to light red-brown	Low	Softwood; excellent for carving. Has visible resin canals.
Western	27	Soft	Moderate; close	Creamy-white to light red-brown	Low	Softwood; good for carving. Has visible resin canals.
Poplar, Yellow	30	Medium hard	Moderate; very close	Canary to brownish-yellow	Good	Easy to cut; finishes well.
Redwood	28	Medium	Pronounced; close	Deep reddish-brown	Low	Softwood. Cuts well but broad spring-summer wood bands limit detail.
Rosewood						
Brazil	50	Hard	Pronounced stripe and swirl with large pores	Mixed browns, purples, blacks	Good	Hard to carve; acts as abrasive on tools. Finishes and burnishes well.
East Indian	55	Hard	Moderate to pronounced	Pinkish to purplish with light and dark streaks	Good	
Satinwood	67	Extremely hard	Moderate; close	Pale gold	Good	Hard to carve, but finishes well.
Spruce	28	Medium	Moderate; close	White through yellow to brown	Low	Softwood; resinous.
Sycamore, American	34	Medium hard	Moderate with pronounced rays; close	Reddish to peach-brown	High	Moderately hard to carve; burnishes well.
Teak	43	Hard	Moderate to pronounced	Yellow-tan through dark-brown with streaks	High	Carves well but is abrasive to tools. Burnishes to waxy luster.
Walnut						
American, black	38	Hard	Moderate to outstanding; close	Light-brown to purple; chocolate-brown	Good	Excellent for carving and finishing. Light sapwood can be darkened by steaming
Claro, (California)	30	Medium hard	Moderate to outstanding; open	Tan to dark-brown with light streaks	Good	
European	34	Medium hard	Moderate to outstanding; open	Tan to dark-brown with light streaks	Good	
Willow	26	Soft	Moderate; close	Creamy to brown	Good	Smooth carving. Burnishes and finishes well.
Zebrawood	48	Hard	Pronounced stripe; close	Pale yellow-tan with dark brown	Good	Moderately hard to carve. Has striped effect.

Tools — Their Use and Care

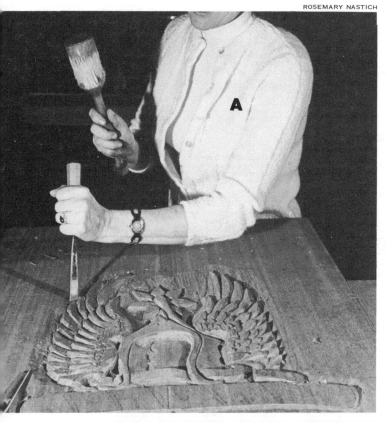

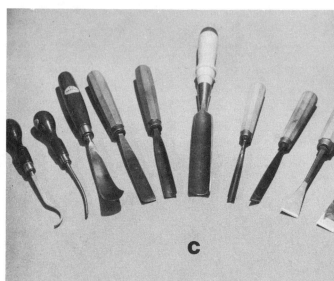

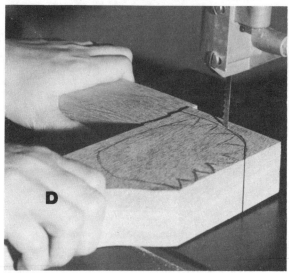

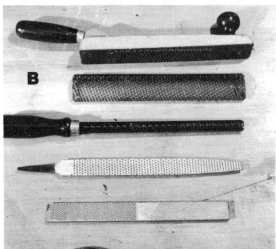

Shown here are some of the most frequently used woodcarving tools—**A**: Gouge and mallet. **B**: Rasps and rifflers. **C**: Chisels. **D**: Bandsaw. **E**: Knife.

You don't need a large and expensive selection of tools to become a successful woodcarver. In fact, you can get started with fewer tools than most other artists and craftsmen require. Untold thousands of exquisite carvings have been made with single and often extremely crude tools, not by choice but simply because those were the best implements available to the carver at the time.

Today's woodcarver can choose from a variety of tools obtainable in a huge selection of sizes and shapes. If you are wise, you will start with a minimum number of tools and add others only as you need them.

The beginner tends to waste time and energy fretting over his choice of tools. One hobbyist spent three years agonizing over, selecting, and eventually buying some forty woodcarver's chisels before even starting to carve. Four years and several carvings later, he realized that he had actually needed only seven of the forty and went looking for special projects that would require the use, and justify the purchase, of the other thirty-three. This sort of thing happens time and again. Don't waste time wondering—start carving, and the necessary tools will soon become obvious.

CHOOSING YOUR EDGE TOOLS

Quality is more important than shape or size—especially in edge tools. Cheap knives and chisels, easily replaced, are extremely expensive in terms of cash, time, and temper. The question of which country produces the best cutting tools can cause a heated discussion at any carvers' meeting. Many believe that handmade Sheffield tools are the finest and hold the best cutting edges. Others maintain the superiority of top-of-the-line German, English, Italian, or Japanese tools. Still others insist that high-grade American tools are as good or better than imported ones.

Whichever you buy, select the best quality you can afford. Actually, the price spread between top-grade and bargain-table types is surprisingly small.

A few standard carpenter's tools—handsaw, plane, square, and steel tape measure—will come in handy for reducing lumber to appropriate shape, size, and surface desired for carving. In addition, you will need a simple coping saw for cutting curves and complicated outlines, and a drill to make holes for any pierced work that may be required. Any other hand or power tools are simply a bonus in working ease, not a necessity.

Knives are probably the most versatile of edge tools, and in one shape or another can be used for most carving except in restricted areas which must be internally carved. Unfortunately, too many woodcarvers consider knives beneath the dignity of a "mallet and chisel" artist. Don't fall into this trap. A small

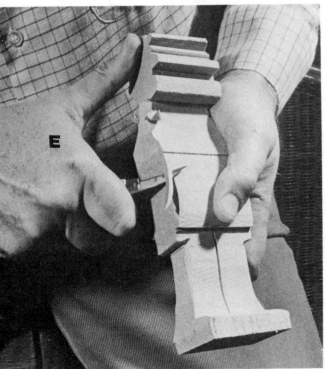

E

CHARLES A. SCHAFFER

There are five basic knife grips from which, as you gain experience, you will develop innumerable variations to suit your own style and preferences.

The forehand grip is used when cutting away from the body. Hold the knife in your clenched fist with the back of the knife cradled in the fleshy pad between your thumb and forefinger. The grip is used

where massive wasting cuts are required to reduce a rough blank to shape.

The draw grip is used where more control is required. With the back of the knife cradled in the second knuckle of your index finger hold the knife in your four fingers, the thumb free. Then, with thumb clasped under the index finger, draw the blade toward you for large wasting cuts. Greater control

for short cuts is obtained by placing the thumb of the other hand on the workpiece ahead of the cutting edge as an anchor point or steady rest and drawing the knife toward the thumb. A secretary's rubber thimble is good thumb insurance here.

The pointer grip (or fishing rod grip) is essentially the same as the draw grip except that the thumb is

used on the side or back of the blade to provide added control for short cuts. With this grip, the thumb of the other hand can be used on the tip of the blade for added force and control.

The dagger grip is a reversal of the draw grip with the thumb over the end of the handle (for long

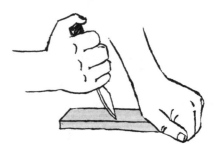

handles, around the handle) and the blade at the bottom of the fist. It is used for deep, heavy cuts.

The pencil grip is used for fine line and detailing work. Hold the knife like a pencil, cutting toward the body. The index finger usually applies the necessary

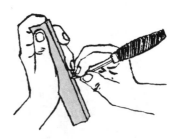

pressure on the back edge, and the other fingers provide support on the workpiece.

Basic Knife Cuts

Knives are used to make seven basic cuts and innumerable personalized variations.

The wedge cut is essentially the cut usually made by a chisel. The cut can be made using the full knife edge, or the tip. For short, controlled cuts, the wedge cut is probably the one most often used. There is no side motion—the wedge shape of the cutting edge cuts and splits the wood fiber, especially for rough shaping utilizing the forehand grip, or for more control with the draw, pointer, and pencil grips.

The seesaw cut is a variation often used when large (usually too large) cuts are attempted and the blade is rocked like a seesaw to magnify the wedging effect.

The slicing cut is like the wedge cut except that the blade is given an end-to-end slicing movement, most often from handle to tip of blade, along with the wedging movement. This takes advantage of the blade's minutely saw-toothed edge to speed cutting. It can be used with the same grips as the wedge cut. *Be careful*—it is easy to slice off more than you intend, so practice control before using this cut on an almost finished piece.

The stop cut (sometimes called the striking or outline cut) is an extremely important cut that will be used time and again in carving with both knives and chisels, so learn it well and you will save many a heartbreak later. It is used as a limiting or outlining cut, to prevent later cuts from splitting the wood.

A stop cut is made with the blade at right angles to the carving surface when a right-angle cut would result in a weakened section of the carved surface—such as in a wood printing block having a narrow, raised line. In such a case, the blade is tilted to produce a widened base for extra strength. The point to remember is that the depth and location of the stop cut helps determine the final shapes in the immediate area. Many workers deliberately place stop cuts slightly to the waste side of the pattern outline to allow for error and retain pattern marks through this step.

The saw cut is seldom used except for cutting through small sections, and consists of simply sawing the cutting edge against the wood as though sawing a board. Very little wedging pressure is applied.

The drilling cut (or tip cut) makes use of the tip of the blade to drill a depression into—or a hole through—the carving surface by pressure and rotation; or sometimes to perform wedging, slicing, and scraping cuts in very small areas.

Scraping with the cutting edge is done to smooth or remove wood that cannot conveniently be removed by cutting. It tends to remove whittling and carving-tool marks and, if done against grain or on soft, fibrous woods, can cause roughness.

A safety tip: Remember that a folding pocket-knife is apt to snap shut and cut your fingers, especially if you wedge the cutting-edge or tip into the wood, then back the blade out of the wood too fast. When the blade wedges in the wood, take your time working it out—save your fingers. Occasionally, when working in burly, knotty, or brittle woods, you may get a knife blade wedged in so tight that any rocking or further wedging will endanger the carving. Prevent splitting by using another knife or chisel to cut down to the blade and release it. Actually, woods of these characteristics are best roughed-out by machine rather than with chisels and knives.

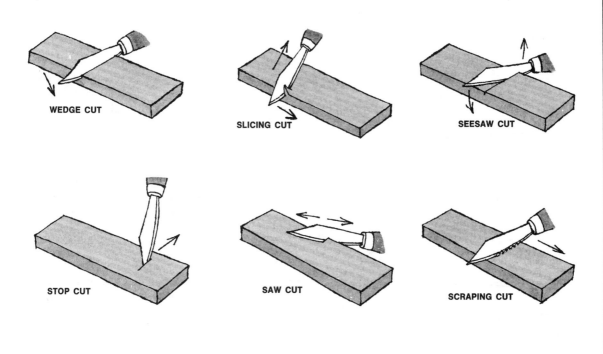

WEDGE CUT   SLICING CUT   SEESAW CUT

STOP CUT   SAW CUT   SCRAPING CUT

DRAW, CURVE BLADE KNIVES are handy for carving intricate shapes and detail for smaller projects.

tip to provide stiffness. This shape is often called a *beak* or, in a longer version with a more shallowly curved back, a *Wharncliffe. Slant tipped* blades serve much the same purposes as sheepfoot tips but are usually thinner and less stiff. *Spear points* are most often used in the form of thin pen blades for fine work. The *spey tip* is virtually the reverse image of the sheepfoot, with the cutting edge on the curve and the heavy spine on the straight edge.

Special shapes produced for carving include a version of the slant tip, called a *skew tip*, in which the slanted tip is sharpened much like a chisel used for chip carving; several angled and curved blades designed for use as draw knives (see photo at left); and the *Indian canoe knife* (see page 17).

Knife blades are customarily sharpened either in V, hollow, or concave cross sections—any of which may or may not have a rolled edge or secondary bevel at the cutting edge. Hollow or concave-ground knives are generally too weak for most woodcarvers

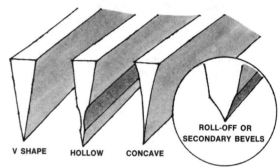

V SHAPE **HOLLOW** **CONCAVE** **ROLL-OFF OR SECONDARY BEVELS**

because of their thin cross sections near the cutting edge. They can, however, be useful for very fine work. The beginner would do well to start with knives in V cross sections and try to stick with them except for heavy-duty blades to be used where heavy prying pressure must be exerted. As you become more experienced, you will very probably make edge shape modifications to suit your own style of work. Most carvers eventually add at least a slight roll to heavier blades to provide better control of the cutting edge. Crisp, unrolled edges cut beautifully but have a tendency to dive into the grain and, being thinner, are more likely to chip under heavy pressure.

Knife blades of special shapes can be cut and ground from saw blades (handsaw and hacksaw), scraper and plane blades, razors, files, and old high-carbon steel butcher knives. (For shaping and heat treating, see pages 21-23).

Firmers and gouges. The term "chisel" denotes any tool with a cutting edge at the end of a blade designed to be pushed or driven forward to chip, cut, dress, or shape metal, stone, or wood. The familiar "carpenter's chisel"—having a straight cutting edge formed by a single bevel—is of use to the woodcarver for jobs similar to carpentry, such as cutting mortises for wood joining.

selection of knives, or a *sturdy* two- or three-bladed pocket knife, is a good starting point for any woodcarver. Learn to sharpen, hone, and use knives, and you are well on your way toward understanding the use of chisels and scrapers. More important, you will get the feel of wood textures, grains, and workability.

Blades are available in a confusing variety of shapes and sizes. However, they break down into five basic shapes—plus a few odd-ball but useful shapes (see sketch). The *clip blade* provides a long, curved cutting edge for general cutting and reaching into restricted areas. The *sheepfoot* has a straight cutting edge with a heavy back curving down to the

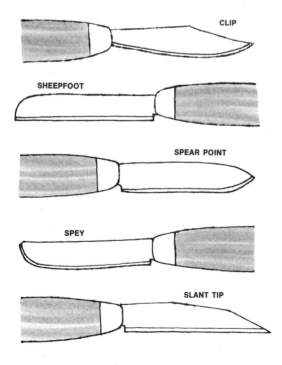

CLIP

SHEEPFOOT

SPEAR POINT

SPEY

SLANT TIP

SPECIAL TOOLS YOU CAN MAKE

The most useful tool you will probably want to make is the Indian canoe knife—the crooked knife which is used as a gouge when whittling. Steel can be any high-carbon tool steel, such as a heavy saw or hacksaw blade, cabinetmaker's scraper blade, plane blade, barber's straight razor, old carbon-steel butcher knives, or files.

Files are probably the simplest to process in the home shop, since they need not be rehardened and tempered after shaping and grinding. To retain a serviceable edge, all the other steels require rehardening and tempering if they are "burned" blue by overheating while grinding, or heated red-hot for bending or shaping.

You can make a crooked knife (see sketches below) from a small flat file (or knife) by heating red hot, cooling, grinding to shape, reheating to red hot, and forging to the desired curve. Heating can be done with propane, acetylene, or gasoline torches, a gas cook stove, or a bed of red-hot charcoal fanned by air from a hair dryer. Forge the curved blade by hammering it over the beak of an anvil or over sections of iron pipe. By using different diameters of pipe, a variety of curves can be accurately made. The original file tang can be retained for mounting your crooked knife in a handle. If epoxy glue is used, the tang can be secured in a hole drilled in an old handle. If epoxy putty is used, a new handle can be molded by forming an epoxy putty sausage in a plastic bag, inserting the knife tang, then shaping the putty by squeezing gently with your hand in the posi-

tion you would normally hold the knife. Allow plenty of time to harden before trimming and smoothing.

Knives can be shaped from old butcher knives, razors, saw blades, or plane blades by careful grinding on belt-grinder, wheel grinder, or cut-off wheel. Use gentle pressure and frequent water-cooling if original temper is to be retained. It takes a lot of cooling time to save the temper but it's worth it, especially for straight-razor steels. If the steel turns blue at any point, it has then lost temper and will have to be rehardened and retempered before use.

Most high-carbon steels can be hardened by heating to a cherry red, then fast-quenching by stirring gently in brine solution—¾ pound rock salt per gallon of water. Temper by first polishing the steel with fine abrasive then heating to approximately 500° F., which will produce a brown to purple oxide film on the polished steel. Then slowly air-cool.

Scrapers for special shapes and uses can be made from the same materials used for knives by grinding to shape and sharpening to a burnished-over edge (see page 23).

Background stamps can be fashioned from round or square steel-bar stock, large nails, or bridge spikes. File or grind the tips to shape. Hardening is not required for most work. For maximum life on hard or abrasive woods, harden high-carbon steel as detailed above. Nails and other low-carbon steel can be casehardened by heating cherry red and immersing in a commercial casehardening powder as directed by the manufacturer.

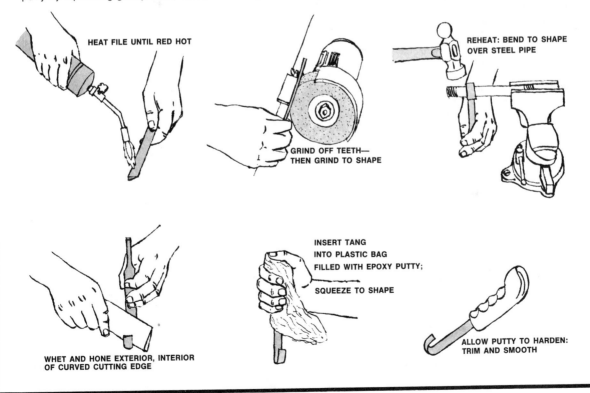

HEAT FILE UNTIL RED HOT

GRIND OFF TEETH—THEN GRIND TO SHAPE

REHEAT: BEND TO SHAPE OVER STEEL PIPE

WHET AND HONE EXTERIOR, INTERIOR OF CURVED CUTTING EDGE

INSERT TANG INTO PLASTIC BAG FILLED WITH EPOXY PUTTY; SQUEEZE TO SHAPE

ALLOW PUTTY TO HARDEN: TRIM AND SMOOTH

There are four basic grips for using wood firmers and gouges.

The single-handed grip (or mallet grip) is used whenever the tool is to be driven by striking with a mallet or palm of the other hand. Grasp the chisel either at or slightly below midpoint (usually with thumb covering the ferrule) somewhat like holding a dagger but with the thumb in line with tool axis. Place cutting

edge on surface and strike end of handle with mallet or hand. The angle of tool to surface, and the force of the blow will largely control appearance and depth of cut.

A **double-handed grip** is used whenever the tool is to be pushed by one hand and guided by the other. Grasp the handle in the right hand (if right handed, that is) as though holding the butt end of a pointer or fishing rod. Grip the blade with the other hand as though holding a dagger, with about 2 to 3 inches projecting below the hand. Place cutting edge on work, adjust to desired angle, push with the upper hand and guide with the lower. Variations in positions of the lower hand and fingers will occur to you

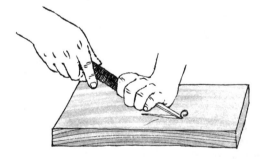

naturally as you progress. You may grasp the blade with only one or two fingers of the lower hand and use the lowest fingers as steady rests or fulcrums for maximum control.

Occasionally an awkward location may require that the upper hand assume a dagger grip with

thumb over top of handle and that the lower hand assume a pencil grip to cut sideways or across your body. Or, both hands may assume the dagger grip, with fingers up and the chisel aimed down or at your body. This is a dangerous direction to cut in, but is sometimes dictated by location. Be extremely careful.

The pencil grip is useful for fine detailing where minimal pressure is needed, and for cleaning up or

making final cuts. Simply hold the blade near the cutting edge as you would a pencil.

The engraver's grip is essentially a one-handed grip in which the blade is held fairly close to the tip, as though holding a pointer or fishing rod. Where a linoleum block tool or wood engraver's burin is used —and the handle is short enough—the end of the

handle is tucked into the heel of the palm. The other hand is used to hold the work and occasionally guide the tip of the cutting tool.

The Six Basic Cuts

There are six cuts commonly made with firmers and gouges plus numerous personalized variations depending on wood, tool, and location.

The stop cut—also called the striking or outline cut —is probably the most important cut in carving. It is used as an initial limiting or outlining cut to prevent later cuts from splitting the wood. The cut is made

THE BASIC GRIPS AND CUTS

with the firmer or gouge held at right angles to the surface or at a slight tilt from right angles to produce a sloping cut which will strengthen the cut edge where a vertically cut edge might chip. The location and depth of a stop cut helps determine the final shape of the pattern at that spot. It is often wise to make the stop cut slightly to the waste side of the pattern outline in order to retain the pattern marks and allow for any finishing cuts.

Firmers or skews are used for cutting straight or nearly straight lines. Curved lines are stop cut by using a gouge having a sweep very nearly matching the curve of the line. It is worth remembering that any gouge can be used to stop cut or outline a circle if you simply slide the edge around in a continuation of its own curve.

The wedge cut is the cut most characteristic of chisels. The mallet grip is used to hold the chisel and the sharpened edge is driven into the wood by striking the end of the handle with mallet or hand. The wedge shape of the edge cuts and splits the wood. Note that without the prior use of the stop cut, the wedge cut can be dangerous to the project because the splitting action can get out of control. Long cuts are made by repeating mallet strikes.

The running cut is a light-weight version of the wedge cut. Instead of being driven by striking with mallet or hand, the firmer or gouge edge is pushed through the wood with steady uninterrupted force. The double-handed grip is used with full-sized tools and the engraver's grip for smaller tools. This cut is used

to make medium to light surface and trimming cuts with firmers and gouges, and to make incisions and grooves with parting tools, fluters, and veiners.

The rocking cut is made by placing one corner of the cutting edge on the work, then rocking the tool along the length of the sharp edge as it is forced into the wood. This cut is used mainly for making short cuts when trimming to layout lines; for cutting across end-grain; cutting straight down into a surface; for along an edge, or at other locations requiring more control than the freehanded running cut.

The slicing cut is made by working the tool so that the cutting edge is worked from one end to the other as it is pushed into the wood. Skews tend naturally to cut in this manner if allowed to slide sideways while being pushed into the work. Firmers are moved with a side-to-side movement while being pushed, often with a fan-like action pivoting around the hand nearest the cutting edge. To achieve a slicing cut with a gouge, the tool must be rotated while being pushed.

Scraping cuts are made using any chisel simply by dragging the sharp edge over the wood surface. The tool edge should be held at a 60° to 90° angle to the surface. Scraping is used to remove only small quantities of material at a single pass, usually in hollowing out or surface finishing operations.

Gouges may be used upside-down with the concave face against the surface, though this is not regarded as a special cut.

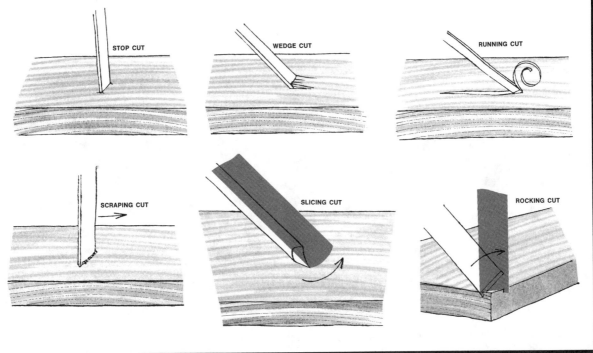

STOP CUT   WEDGE CUT   RUNNING CUT

SCRAPING CUT   SLICING CUT   ROCKING CUT

The true woodcarver's "chisel" is more properly called a *firmer* and has a double bevel forming a straight cutting edge. When the cutting edge is not at right angles to the tool axis, it is known as a *skew firmer.* It should be noted that many experienced carvers make use of carpenter's chisels but almost invariably modify them to semi-firmer or bullnose shapes.

Gouges are simply chisels having curved cutting edges varying from almost flat sweeps or curves (*slow* or *flat gouges*) through semi-circles (*quick gouges*). When the semi-circles are extended to form a U shape, they are called *veiners* in very small sizes and *fluters* in larger radii. "Parting tools" are V-shaped gouges of varying angular cross-sections and widths.

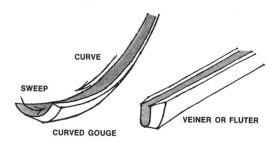

Most firmers and gouges are usually available in bent or curved blade design as well as straight. A gouge is known as a *long-bent* or *grounder* if of shallow blade curvature (not cutting edge) and a *short bent* if sharply curved. When ordering from catalogues, remember that nomenclature is not uniform among manufacturers; therefore, be careful to double check dimensions and shapes.

Most manufacturers offer a starter set of six or seven firmers and gouges assembled in a kit. These are useful to beginning carvers in terms of blade sizes and shapes, but often contain one or more seldom-used shapes. If you start with a kit, buy further shapes and sizes only as you need them and as your experience dictates. Avoid the small, short or mushroom-handled linoleum-block-type carving tools unless very small work or woodcuts are your only goal.

A good starter selection may include a ⅝-inch No. 1 firmer chisel, ⅜-inch No. 39 parting tool, ¾-inch No. 5 straight gouge, ⅝-inch No. 3 straight gouge, ⅝-inch No. 7 straight gouge, ½-inch No. 18 bent gouge, ⅜-inch No. 2 skew firmer, and a small ¼-inch fluter. Tool lengths including handles should not be less than seven inches for best control. Handle shape is a matter of personal choice, but octagonal handles twist less in the hand and roll around less on the bench. Handles should be of a dense hardwood such as boxwood, dogwood, or maple and have brass ferrules to keep handles from splitting when being mallet driven.

Rasps and rifflers are many-toothed, file-like abrasive tools designed for (depending on size and number of teeth) coarsely shaping or smoothing a surface. *Rasps* are available in flat, half-round, and round cross sections and are shaped much like a

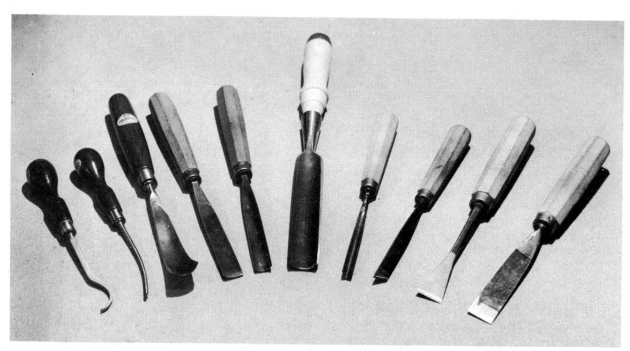

CHISEL STYLES are varied; shown here are (from left) 3/16-inch short bent firmer, ¼ and 1-inch bent gouges, ¾-inch gouge, ⅝-inch quick gouge, 1-inch gouge, ⅜-inch parting tool, ½-inch skew, and 1-inch fishtail, firmer.

standard file. *Rifflers* are usually designed to give a smoother finish than rasps and faintly resemble canoe paddles. The ends are available in many shapes to fill almost every need, from knife-edged to almost hemispherical. *Caution: Many rifflers are extremely brittle, so be gentle—let only the tips of the teeth do the cutting.*

Don't dismiss rasps and rifflers as too simple to be worth using. Many beautiful sculptures have been created by rasps alone. The rasp is an ideal carving tool on which to start a young child, since it often permits beautiful results with minimum training.

The patented industrial-age version of the rasp, made of stamped and formed sheet metal with sharpened teeth, which each look like a midget plane blade, is much easier to use than the traditional chip-toothed rasp and provides a smoother finish.

Scrapers are extremely useful for smoothing surfaces where a clear, unsanded look is desired and can often be used to perform as freehand planer blades to scratch or scrape grooves or shapes. Rectangular and curved scrapers, of standard shapes and sizes, are available at larger hardware and woodworking supply houses. (Special scraper shapes can be made using the techniques described on page 17).

Planes, such as those used by carpenters, are handy for truing up woodcarving blanks prior to actual carving.

KEEPING YOUR EDGE TOOLS IN CONDITION

Sharpening of edge tools is the most important preparation for woodcarving you can make. A dull cutting edge will create more problems for the carver than virtually any other carving fault. Contrary to common belief, a sharper tool is necessary for a soft wood like pine than for a harder wood such as teak— though the sharpest possible is best for both. A dull edge is usually stopped dead in a hard wood but in a soft one it is pushed on through, leaving torn fibers in its wake. A sharp edge makes a whistling sound when cutting across the grain on pine. A dull one makes a chipping, tearing sound. Keep a piece of pine next to your oil stones for a handy test.

Dull edges are considerably more dangerous than sharp ones, simply because more pressure is required to bulldoze them through the material, and if they pass through suddenly the extra pressure can result in serious cuts in hands, legs, etc. A sharp tool needs minimal pressure, is far easier to control, and therefore far safer to handle. Protect edges from damage by storing tools in a fitted cloth roll or in a tool box with specific slots for each tool. Check all edges at the beginning and end of each carving

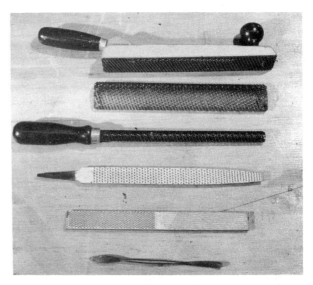

RASPS AND RIFFLERS have flat, curved, round, and half-round shapes; abrasive surfaces range from coarse to fine.

session and repair or resharpen defects immediately.

When using wheels, band grinders, bench stones, or slip stones, the most efficient sharpening occurs as the wheel or abrasive band surface is made to move into the cutting edge. If a bench or slip stone

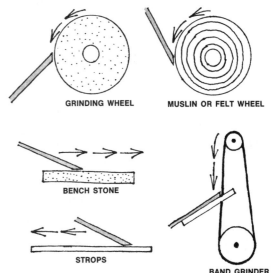

GRINDING WHEEL   MUSLIN OR FELT WHEEL

BENCH STONE

STROPS

BAND GRINDER

is used, the blade is moved with the cutting edge forward. *Caution:* There are important exceptions. On any material readily cut by a sharp edge, such as leather strops or hones, cloth or felt wheels, or resilient-backed slickem-sharps (see page 24), draw the blade across the surface *away* from the sharp edge. Also, some workers prefer to work gouges side to side on bench stones instead of rocking them while running them the length of the stone.

The process of sharpening may be broken down into 4 steps: grinding, whetting, honing, and stropping. Different tools or abrasives are used at each stage. Only for grinding is a power tool almost a necessity—though it can be accomplished manually with determination.

Grinding is traditionally done on a water-cooled, slow-speed (150 rpm), large-diameter sandstone wheel; or on a high-speed (3,450 rpm), small-diameter emery wheel. The sandstone wheels are increasingly difficult to find but allow a good job of sharpening, though the process can be tedious. High-speed emery wheels are fast but tricky. They build up heat extremely fast in the blade being ground, and will ruin the temper of the steel if extreme care is not

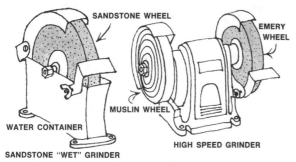

SANDSTONE WHEEL
EMERY WHEEL
MUSLIN WHEEL
WATER CONTAINER
SANDSTONE "WET" GRINDER
HIGH SPEED GRINDER

taken to cool the blade. Frequent dipping in cool water is necessary.

A third alternative is the band grinder/sander. It is a skinny (usually 1 inch), upright version of the belt sander crossed with a bandsaw. The advantages of a band sander are many. First, it grinds a tool with much less danger of overheating the blade. Second, it can continue the process of sharpening by whetting

BAND GRINDER can grind, whet, and hone tools quickly and safely; is also used to shape and sand carvings.

and honing (see the next two pages) the tool using successively finer grit bands. Thirdly, it can perform most of the other specialized workshop functions of a wheel grinder and yet does a great job as a band sander on carving and general shop projects.

Grind chisel edges to the correct shape before grinding a bevel edge. Thus, a carpenter's chisel or firmer edge must be at right angles to the axis of the tool; a skew edge would be at any predetermined angle to the axis (often 60° or 45° from the axis); a gouge or any other shaped tool must be shaped so that the entire cutting edge will contact a squared piece of wood resting on a table when the tool is held against it in a normal cutting position. For tools

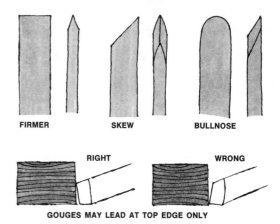

FIRMER   *SKEW*   *BULLNOSE*
RIGHT   *WRONG*
GOUGES MAY LEAD AT TOP EDGE ONLY

intended for work on hard woods, use a larger bevel angle than for softer woods.

Always grind the edge (at point of contact) exactly parallel to the axle of the wheel (on band grinders, to the axle of the drive wheel). This will produce an even bevel. With gouges, the tool will have to be rocked or turned evenly during grinding, and parting tools (particularly if bent) may have to be held at apparently odd angles to keep the edge parallel to the axle. It sounds a great deal harder to do than it

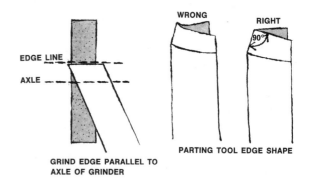

WRONG   *RIGHT*
90°
EDGE LINE
AXLE
PARTING TOOL EDGE SHAPE
GRIND EDGE PARALLEL TO AXLE OF GRINDER

actually is, but it is well worth some practice with scrap pieces of pipe or steel bar to save valuable knife or chisel edges. Start with a medium-grit wheel or belt and progress in two or more steps to finer grits.

Grind plane blades like single-bevel carpenter's chisels. In those cases where the plane does not use a breaker plate on the blade assembly, a very short bevel or rolloff on the top edge will assist the blade in breaking and clearing wood chips.

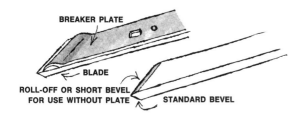

This breaker bevel, or roll-off, is also used by many carvers on the inner faces of gouges and parting tools, and the normally unbeveled side of carpenter's chisels (an especially useful form of which is the bull-nosed or round-nosed chisel). It permits better chip clearing, and when the tool is reversed to straddle and cut a raised design (like grapes or branches using the inner face of a gouge), there is better control and less tendency to dive into the grain.

Scraper edges for larger scrapers are usually ground and whetted square, then burnished over to provide a cutting wire-edge on both edges, thus making them reversible. Smaller and non-reversible scrapers are often ground to a single bevel having an included angle between 30° and 90°, depending

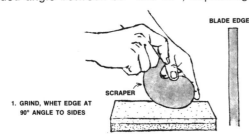

1. GRIND, WHET EDGE AT 90° ANGLE TO SIDES

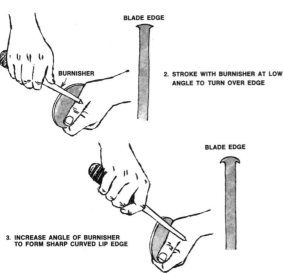

2. STROKE WITH BURNISHER AT LOW ANGLE TO TURN OVER EDGE

3. INCREASE ANGLE OF BURNISHER TO FORM SHARP CURVED LIP EDGE

on the shape of the area to be scraped and the shape of the tool itself. The sharp edge is then burnished over.

Grind axes, hatchets, and adzes (useful for roughing out shapes) to more of a V-edge than originally provided. The woodcarver usually grips these tools close to the head for best control. Sculptor's adzes are available at a few mail-order, hardware, and sculptor's supply houses. A serviceable one can be made by modifying the cutting edge on a bricklayer's hammer or a small pick-mattock. When grinding an

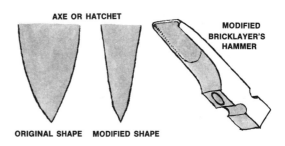

adze's edge, form a shallow-curved, gouge-like edge instead of a square one, and you will have fewer problems with edge-splitting and hogging-into the grain.

Whetting can be performed on the band grinder/sander or on a bench stone. Most carvers agree that the best natural whetting stone is *Washita* (which will probably have to be specially ordered from your supplier). *Slip stones*, which are simply specially-shaped pieces of natural or manufactured stones, can be used to simplify the whetting and honing (see below) of the inner faces of gouges, fluters, veiners, parting tools, and their relatives. They are readily available with curved and knife edges, with curved or V-shaped grooves, and in triangular, round, and rat-tailed shapes. Manmade stones in medium to fine

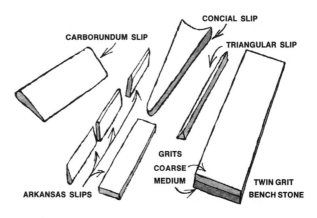

grades are faster cutting and easier to obtain than *Washita* and probably do as good a job. Use the liquid recommended by the manufacturer on all bench stones. The purpose is not to lubricate the surface, but to lift and carry metal particles out of the stone's grain structure where they could impede the cutting action. A mixture of equal parts kerosene and high-grade non-detergent No. 10 motor oil works in most cases, but follow the maker's instructions if possible. Always keep unused stones covered and moist, but wiped free of excess oil. Clean them periodically using the method recommended by the manufacturer: for natural stone, it is usually a kerosene wash; for manufactured stones, heating in an oven until they sweat old oil, then wiping dry while still hot.

Whet all ground edges on a fine band-grinder belt (using the same techniques as for grinding) or whet the edge on a bench stone. To whet an edge on a bench stone, align the axis of the tool with the length of the stone, lay straight-beveled edges flat on the stone, and work the edge the length of the stone until the edge appears uniform and has no flat spots on the cutting edge. Then raise the back edge of the bevel approximately 15° for knives and 20° to 25° for chisels, and continue to work the length of the stone until a secondary bevel and sharp edge is produced. Firmers will have to have both front and back face bevels equally sharpened. Gouges must be evenly rocked while holding at the correct angles

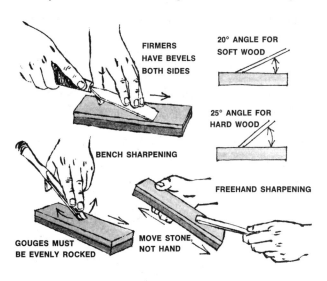

FIRMERS HAVE BEVELS BOTH SIDES

20° ANGLE FOR SOFT WOOD

25° ANGLE FOR HARD WOOD

BENCH SHARPENING

GOUGES MUST BE EVENLY ROCKED

MOVE STONE, NOT HAND

FREEHAND SHARPENING

and worked the length of the stone. Some carvers prefer to work gouges sideways down the length of the stone while rocking.

Although straight-line manipulation of tools on bench-mounted stones is probably the safest for the beginner, at least two other methods are used by some experienced pattern makers and carvers.

The first variation is simply to move the tool in a figure-eight pattern on the stone surface instead of working in a straight line from end to end. The main disadvantage to the novice is a tendency to inadvertently round off corners on firmers and skews.

Also, the technique may develop a depression in the stone faster than would the end-to-end method.

The second variation is the freehand one favored by many experienced pattern makers and carvers. The chisel is held pointer-fashion in the left hand (assuming the worker is right-handed) with the elbow braced against the body—or against the bench. The stone is gripped in the right hand and worked against the stationary tool. There are two disadvantages to this method: Careless handling of the stone can lead to cut fingers on the right hand, and allowing the angle of the stone to vary while in motion can result in misshaped bevels. Both problems can be overcome by care and a little practice.

V-shaped parting tools present a particular problem. The point of the V must be kept sharp and must not lead or lag behind the cutting edge.

The inner faces of gouges and parting tools are whetted with appropriately shaped slip-stones.

Honing is usually best performed on a natural hard Arkansas stone, a "slickem-sharp," or an abrasive-loaded strop. (See next page for instructions on making slickem-sharps and strops.) Hard Arkansas stones are available at most hardware stores. Abrasive-loaded strops can be made in the home workshop, or superb ones loaded with diamond dust can be obtained from a medical/scientific supply house where they are sold as replacements for microtome knife hones.

Hone on bench stones (usually hard Arkansas) using precisely the same methods as for whetting but concentrate on the secondary bevel to eliminate any wire edges. Power honing on abrasive-loaded cloth or felt wheels is done in the reverse position from grinding; that is, with the edge dragging instead of facing into the wheel rotation. Similarly, when using an abrasive-loaded honing strop, drag the edge across the strop instead of pushing it edge first, as you would on a stone.

Stropping is most often done on a strip of leather similar to the razor strops used by old-time barbers.

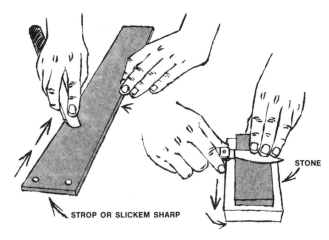

STROP OR SLICKEM SHARP

STONE

Many experienced carvers find that a two or three-stage stropping works best: first on a strop loaded with jeweler's rouge, then on a plain leather strop, finally in the palm of the hand.

A very effective honing/stropping operation is possible if you have a rotating spindle such as a wheel grinder, drill motor, etc. Use a firmly-stitched cloth buffing wheel loaded with a medium-fine buffing compound for honing, and a firmly-stitched muslin wheel or a solid felt wheel loaded with rouge or stainless steel buffing compound for final machine stropping.

All stropping, powered or hand, is performed with the edge dragging against the abrasive.

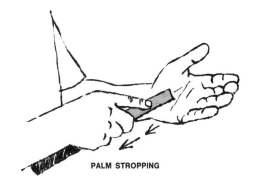

PALM STROPPING

SLICKEM-SHARPS AND STROPS

Seldom used by the home craftsman or carver are two sharpening devices often used by whittlers and barbers: the "slickem-sharp" and the strop.

Simple to make and use, you will never want to be without a slickem-sharp once you've used one. Start with a stick of wood, add an ⅛-inch layer of sponge (not foam) rubber, inner tube rubber, or resilient felt; then stretch and tack a strip of abrasive cloth over the padded stick. Use a flat stick for sharpening knives, firmers, and the outer edges of gouges. A round, oval, or knife-edged stick is used for gouges, veiners, fluters, crooked knives, or any other tool with a curved or angled inner edge. Individual carvers differ on the best grit size, choices ranging from 120 to 320-grit. A good starting point is 180-grit aluminum oxide cloth.

Strops come in two varieties: abrasive-loaded fabric (or leather) and unloaded leather. Abrasive-loaded strops are made either of heavy leather or of cotton webbing or belting. A buffing compound, or jeweler's rouge in a wax or oil base, is rubbed into the strop surface in an amount depending on the degree of cutting desired from the abrasive.

The cotton-webbing strop tends to hold an abrasive load longer because of the reservoirs formed by the weave. A similar effect can be obtained in leather by first spiking the surface with the point of a six-penny nail to form a pockmark pattern, with pits spaced approximately 1/10-inch apart. Then load abrasive grit on the surface and into the spiked holes, and rub in the desired amount of buffing compound. A variation is to use a thin, flexible glue (instead of wax or oil), work the mixture into the leather, squeeze the surface clear of any excess abrasive and glue, and allow to dry.

Unloaded strops are made of very high-quality, heavy, supple leather and used for final polish only.

Some workers place a slickem-sharp and a strop on opposite sides of a single wooden stick. Ordinarily, strops tend to stay cleaner and last longer if kept separate from each other and apart from slickem-sharps and all other abrasives.

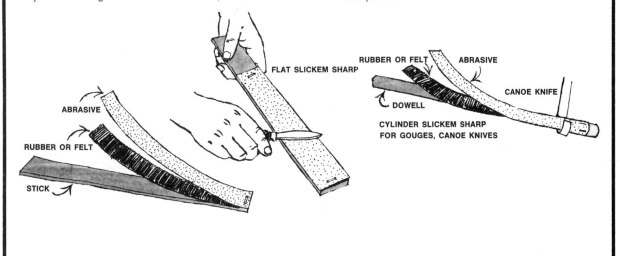

FLAT SLICKEM SHARP

ABRASIVE

RUBBER OR FELT

STICK

RUBBER OR FELT   ABRASIVE

DOWELL

CANOE KNIFE

CYLINDER SLICKEM SHARP
FOR GOUGES, CANOE KNIVES

POWER TOOLS

Traditionalists sometimes regard the use of power tools in woodcarving as unprofessional. But a growing number of sculptors and carvers believe that the best available tool for a given job should be used, whether power or hand tool. Don't use power tools if you regard them as inartistic, but don't feel that they are forbidden or less than honest.

Drills, whether portable or drill press, are extremely useful for removing waste wood in areas to be hollowed out (using Forstner-type bits or end mills); and are equally handy for powering flexible shafts and sanding discs, drums, and brush-backed flap sanders.

Power saws are invaluable for shaping and preparing wood for carving. *Portable, bench,* and *radial circular* saws are very useful as straight line cutters on planks up to a maximum of 4 inches thick. *Jig* and *sabre* saws perform well at straight and curved cutting on wood up to 2 or 3 inches thick. *Band saws* can handle straight and curved cutting to a maximum of 6 or 12 inches thick (depending on the saw).

Don't overlook the possibilities of power saws for cutting, trimming, and slicing green logs, and for rough—even final—shaping of large projects.

Especially handy are reciprocating saws, which resemble toothy handsaws—but with powerful electric or gasoline motors mounted at, or just ahead of, the handle. These are essentially straight-line cutters and are excellent for slicing up small logs to size. Electric versions are useful for many carpentry and framing jobs and are acceptably quiet for indoor use.

Chain saws, available in either electric or gasoline powered models, are highly portable and extremely useful woodcutting and carving instruments.

Even with one of the lightest-weight units, you can remove wood faster than with a chisel. A large unit makes for faster primary cutting and slicing, but doesn't save enough time in hollowing or slotting to compensate for its extra weight, in the long run. Gasoline saws are dependable, though noisy for indoor use. Inexpensive electric chain saws intended for occasional odd jobs seldom hold up well in carving use.

Sanders of the finishing variety—such as pad and belt sanders—are useful in initial preparation for carving, and occasionally in final finishing and installation. Disc and drum sanders are primarily used for edge sanding. The band grinder/sander described on page 22 is excellent for sanding and shaping operations. The brush-backed flap sander is ideal for surface finishing of irregular surfaces;

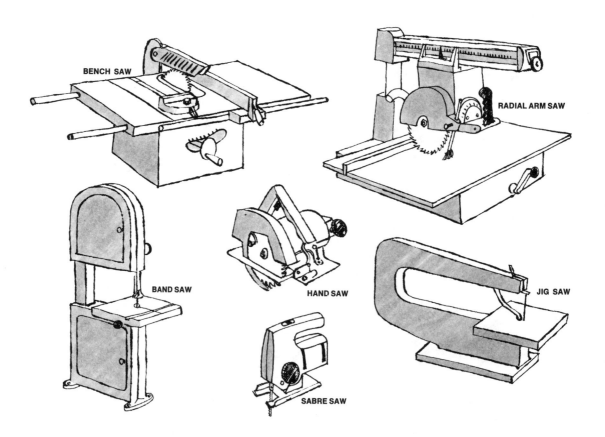

BENCH SAW

RADIAL ARM SAW

BAND SAW

HAND SAW

JIG SAW

SABRE SAW

RECIPROCATING HANDSAW does fast, efficient rough cutting of green logs into shapes for seasoning, carving.

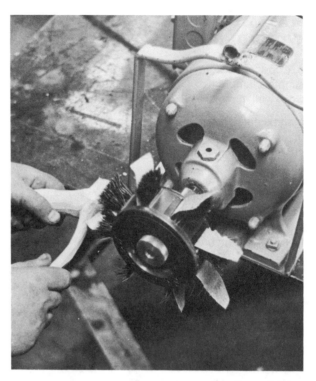

FLAP SANDERS with brush-backed abrasive strips are good for smoothing complex shapes with speed, control.

by using 1-inch-wide abrasive strips slit into ⅛-inch-wide sub-strips, very fine detail can be finished.

Hand grinders, ranging from lightweight but amazingly powerful ultracompact, high rpm models with permanent magnet DC motors to heavier industrial types having considerably more power, fulfill a number of carving functions using rotary burrs, rasps, and router bits. The lighter weight ones can be handled freehand, but the heavier ones work best in a horizontal or vertical bench mount, where the work can be moved against the bits. Full wave, solid state speed controls, often obtainable from the grinder manufacturers, can be used to control tool speeds from zero to as high as 25,000 to 30,000 rpm. Router motors make good high-speed, high-powered, bench-mounted grinders.

For detail work, the greatest convenience is provided by a variable speed motor driving a flexible shaft with interchangeable hand pieces able to take cutters with shanks from ⅛ through ¼ inch.

Grinder and flexible shaft-driven burrs, rasps, and bits make it easy to remove large quantities of wood rapidly, yet offer sureness of control that enables even the beginner to equal the detail created by more experienced carvers, and allow the professional to achieve delicacy and intricacy of detail with speed and ease. Power carving is especially useful on tough or abrasive woods which quickly dull cutting edges, and woods having curly, unpredictable grains.

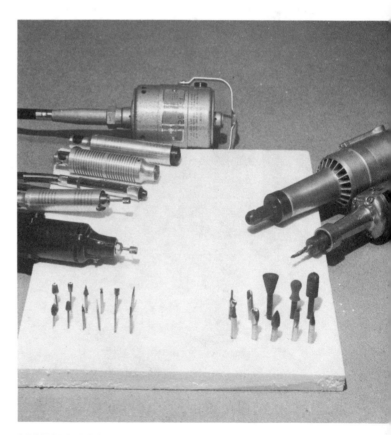

GRINDERS, BITS are varied in sizes, shapes. For fine detail, use grinder with speed control, flexible shaft.

MALLETS, CLAMPS, AND WORKBENCHES

A woodcarver's mallet for striking edge tools, a few simple clamping devices, and a bench on which to work will be extremely helpful to the woodcarver.

Mallets for woodcarving are usually of the potato-masher variety. It may seem odd to use a curved striking surface, but a little comparative practice will soon convince you that you will make fewer mistakes with the potato-masher type of mallet than with a standard carpenter's, mechanic's, or cooper's mallet. The heads are usually of beech, hickory, or lignum vitae (in ascending order of weight). Lengths vary from 7 to 12 inches, diameters from 2½ to 7 inches, and weights from 6 to 32 ounces. Fairly good light-weight mallets can be made from broken baseball bats, hardwood lawn mower rollers, and rolling pins.

Clamping and holding devices for assembling, laminating, and carving wood are extremely varied in size, shape, and use. Basic styles include the familiar woodworker's bench vise and associated bench stops, *parallel-jaw wood clamps, C-clamps,* and *bar clamps.* Less familiar are *bench holdfasts, carver's screws* and *screw clamps, turn buttons, dogs,* and *locks,* all of which use a screw or bar to hold the work firmly to the bench top. A handy, ready-made bench dog can be obtained from an auto parts house or garage: Ask for one of the horseshoe-shaped clamps used to hold auto distributors in place.

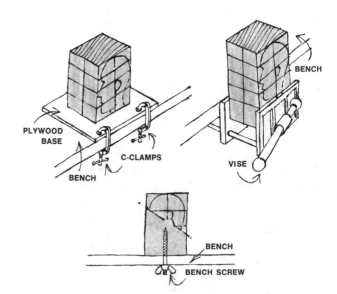

If clamps interfere with carving operations, it is common practice to first attach the work piece to a sheet of plywood with glue or screws. An old wood-turner's trick worth trying is to use thick, brown bag paper or slick magazine cover paper as a spacer, and white-glue it between work and clamp board. The work piece will hold through the heaviest tool pressures, yet can be later separated from the heavy paper with a thin, stiff knife blade.

A workbench, for anything but whittling, woodcuts, and very small pieces, must be sturdy enough not to vibrate and walk under the heavy pressure of mallet work. It should be at a comfortable height for most of the work you plan to do; a widely accepted standard places the top surface of the bench at about the level of the carver's hip bone. A standard woodworker's bench with vise is fine, if sturdy and high enough. If you intend to do much large sculpture in-the-round (see pages 56-61), you might consider a pedestal-type bench having a 12 to 24-inch square top and a base heavily weighted with rock, bags of dry cement, scrap iron, or any other heavy material. Your bench should, if practical, be fastened to the floor and made of the heaviest practical materials, both for strength and stability and to reduce impact noise when using the mallet. Lightweight steel cabinet-based benches can be especially noisy.

Auxiliary equipment for benches should include one or more pieces of carpet—preferably densely woven, wool plush pile—to hold panels in place without clamping and to protect workpiece surfaces; a heavy canvas bag approximately 20 by 30 inches and two-thirds filled with sand, used to cradle odd shaped pieces on the bench top as needed; holes drilled in bench top to receive bench stop-pegs and bar type hold-fasts; a bench stone and strop slide or drawer, plus one or more tool drawers.

MALLET HEAD (right) has curved striking surface; light-weight mallet (left) can be made from rolling pin.

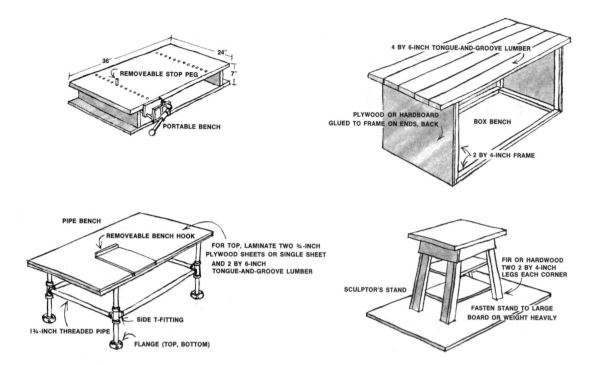

WORKBENCH DIMENSIONS can be tailored to your waist height and arm reach. Bench tops can be of laminated plywood or edge-glued 2 by 4's or 2 by 6's. Walkboard is optional if sculptor's stand is weighted heavily.

HOW TO MAKE SPRING CLAMPS

An extremely useful type of clamp for fine assembly or repair work is the spring-wire clamp. It is simply made from spring-wire or sections cut from upholstery springs. A pair of large, narrow-waisted upholstery springs will supply enough material for a dozen or more clamps in several sizes.

Where surface dents in the wood are unimportant, you may leave the wire ends as cut, or you can either grind them to a point or round them off, as you prefer. Sharp points are excellent for holding miters and other slippery joints. To prevent surface marring, simply attach a wood chip to the block of wood with doublefaced tape before your applying of the clamp.

Cut and bend wires to the shapes shown. Using a clamp for work smaller than optimum provides insufficient pressure, and on larger work provides a twisting force that is hard to control.

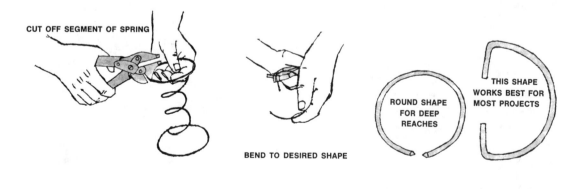

Carved Surface Decoration

ALEXANDER ZELLER

JOSEPH SENEY

HAZEL A. DIEPEN

Methods used for *carvings shown here are—*
A: Incised and chip. B: Low relief. C: Low relief
and incised. D: Incised. E: Intaglio and incised.

ELFREDA
ZELLER

Surface decoration is probably the oldest and simplest form of decorative carving and requires less practiced awareness of proportion and space than carving in-the-round. Modern variations of this early technique are to be found in scrimshaw (nautical ivory carving), woodcuts, wood engravings, and chip carving. Of these, *chip carving* is probably easiest for the beginner—all you need is a knife or single-edge razor blade and a block of medium to soft wood, such as basswood or pine. Chip carving's popularity lies in its comparative simplicity of technique, the speed with which surfaces can be carved, and the

fact that patterns may be readily developed from either geometric or natural figures.

CHIP CARVING

The process of cutting triangular, wedge-shaped chips from a wood surface is called *chip carving*. The thickest part of the chip is at the apex of the triangle and the thinnest portion along the base. This basic shape may be varied simply by changing the relative dimensions of the triangles or curving one or more of the sides—even using semi-circles or lip shapes. You can then combine any of the resulting forms into original patterns of your own.

As important as design to the final effect are the dividers between chips and the crisp, clean appearance of the cut surfaces.

Tools for chip carving can vary widely depending on the experience and preference of the carver. Many woodworkers use standard carving chisels. Many others use chip-carving knives, pocket knives, single-edge razor blades, and utility knives. The beginner should be wary of chisels until he gains experience with knives, the craft itself, and the feel of knife-on-wood. There are two basic knife shapes: striking and slicing (also called sticking and splitting). These are simply specialized versions of skew-chisel and sheepfoot blades (see page 16). Most chip carvers use one variation or another of these two basic shapes for specific needs.

In the instructions that follow, it is assumed that the striking knife will be used when the instruction is "to strike" a line, and the slicing knife when the instruction is "to slice". If this seems elementary, remember that in fact either operation can be performed with any suitable blade—though with some decrease in ease of operation. The striking cut is essentially a stop or outline cut (see page 15).

ARNIE GARBORG

Single basic triangles are cut by striking along a line AB with the deepest point at A and the blade surfacing at B. Ensure a strong cut edge by tilting the blade 10° to 15° from the vertical, forming a slight slope in the cutout instead of a sharply vertical edge which is likely to flake or chip under handling. Repeat along line AC. Then slice along line

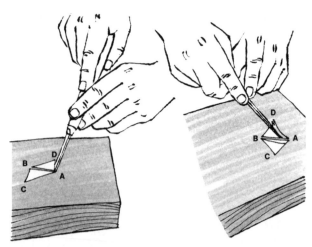

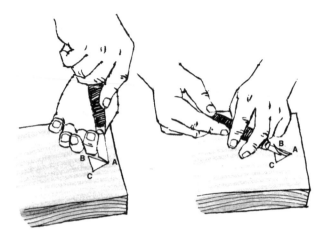

BC with the blade angled to match the slope of striking cuts made along lines AB and AC.

Multiple basic triangles are each cut exactly like the single basic triangle, *except* that the angle of

COMPOUND TRIANGLES, roughly cut, make up this unusual design; can be combined with other surface cuts.

the striking cut is especially important where the dividers between triangles are used.

Compound triangles are cut as though they are three smaller triangles included (without dividers) within a large triangle. Strike along lines AB, AC, and AD. Strike *vertically* since there will be no edges left along these lines. Slice along lines BC, CD, and DB as for the single triangle. Care must be taken to

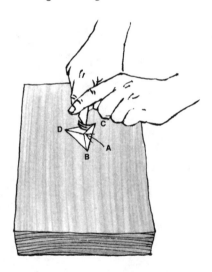

match the slopes of the striking cuts with the depth of the three slicing cuts so that they meet evenly for most designs. Occasionally, the sliced surfaces are deliberately cut to three different levels for specific effects. Used carelessly, multi-level cutting looks overly busy and confusing.

Lip or V-cuts are simply straight or curved cuts having V-shaped cross sections with the base line of the V rising to the surface at each end of the cut. Lay out the outer edges of the cut (labeled B and C respectively), then locate a center or depth-of-cut line (labeled A). Line A is usually centered between lines B & C but for special effects may be off-centered or even made to wander from side to side.

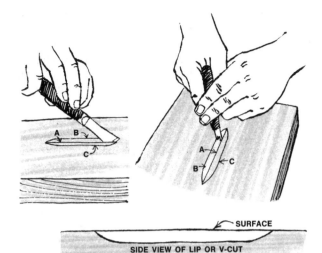

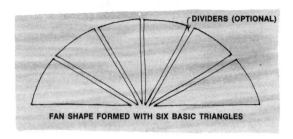

Fan and circular shapes are formed by grouping any of the above cuts around a focal point.

DIVIDERS (OPTIONAL)

FAN SHAPE FORMED WITH SIX BASIC TRIANGLES

SURFACE

SIDE VIEW OF LIP OR V-CUT

INCISED LINE CARVING

Cutting incisions or grooves into a surface to outline forms is known as *incised line carving*. The outlined form and background remain at the original level. The grooves usually have U or V-shaped cross sections, although any shape may be used. Wood blocks, engravings, and incised lettering are examples of incised line carving.

Since grooves are to be produced, you have two choices. You can select the appropriately shaped gouge, fluter, veiner, or parting tool and start cutting (see the section on cutting with chisels and gouges, pages 18 and 19); or you can use a variation of the chip carver's method for making a lip cut.

(Only vary from the center for specific, controlled effects.) Strike the line A so that the depth of cut is uniform except at the two ends, where the cut rises to the surface. Slice along lines B and C, angling the blade toward the bottom of the line A.

A special case of the off center depth-of-cut (line A) is the half-V or half-lip cut, in which only a single

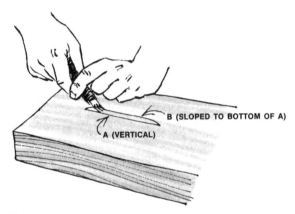

B (SLOPED TO BOTTOM OF A)

A (VERTICAL)

slicing cut is made along only one side of line A. The striking cut is usually made at a 10° to 15° angle in this case to strengthen the cut edge.

Single ended lip cuts are simply lip or V-cuts that have, in effect, been chopped in half lengthwise and have only a single pointed end. The blunt end may be either a vertical cut or an angled slice.

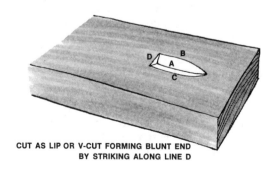

CUT AS LIP OR V-CUT FORMING BLUNT END
BY STRIKING ALONG LINE D

TEEN BECKSTED COLLECTION

INCISED LINE DESIGNS similar to one shown here on Indian printing block are used to decorate fabrics.

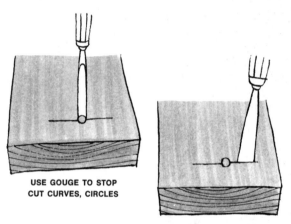

In the hands of an expert, the direct carving sweep with fluter, veiner, or parting tool is a thing of beauty to behold. But most beginners have trouble with these tools until they gain experience, so don't feel clumsy if you have troubles at first. Fortunately, there is an alternate method that uses these tools for final trim only.

Lay out the grooves exactly as for the lip or V-cut (page 32). Strike or stop cut (page 15) along the centerline with a vertically held knife, firmer, or gouge. Straight lines should be stop cut with firmer or knife, and curves cut with gouges having sweeps matching the line curves. Make the stop cut slightly shallower than the desired final depth to allow for final trimming. Use the appropriate firmer or gouge to make an angled cut from just inside one of the outer layout lines toward the bottom of the stop cut.

USE GOUGE TO STOP CUT CURVES, CIRCLES

USE FIRMER OR SKEW TO STOP CUT STRAIGHT LINES

SPANISH TRAY has incised floral design and scalloped background (see page 47 for detailed instructions).

Repeat on other side of centerline. This produces a V-shaped groove which is then trimmed to final cross section with fluter, veiner, or parting tool.

INCISED CARVING

This type of carving is the more ornate brother of incised *line* carving. The differences are that in incised carving, the outlined shapes may be modeled or carved; the background side of the outer outlining groove is often broadly dished to emphasize separation between the outlined shape and the background; and the background surface may be shallowly tool-marked with gouges of fairly flat sweep.

INTAGLIO CARVING

Intaglio is probably most often seen in the form of butter or cooky molds used to form patterns in relief on butter or cooky surfaces. The signet ring is a more ornate example of intaglio, which is simply the

If you have the correct size and shape gouge, fluter, veiner, or parting tool to suit the job, clamp the work to the bench and proceed with care. Don't try to cut the groove in one pass. Make a series of passes, removing small portions of wood each time. Fluters, veiners, and parting tools have a tendency to try to "run-up-track" with the grain and get out of

WORK CAREFULLY TO AVOID "RUNNING UP TRACK" AND CHIPPED EDGES

control when cutting across the grain or diagonally to it. Practice on scrap wood of a similar type will save much valuable wood, time, and temper on the actual project. Wherever practical, cut across the grain or diagonally before cutting with the grain— this will minimize chipped edges at intersections. Running a stop cut down the centerline of the groove is often helpful in controlling the tools when cutting diagonally or across the grain.

INTAGLIO PANEL is carved with gouges of varying sizes; panel is then fittted in place as part of door decoration. Carving could also be done directly on the door surface.

negative or reverse form of relief carving. Melted wax poured into an intaglio carving will set to form a perfectly-shaped relief model of the intaglio-carved subject. Intaglio is produced largely with gouges of various sizes and sweeps, though knives, small skews, firmers, and parting tools may be useful for detailing. Intaglio may be as simple as single-depth incised line carving, such as is often used for initial seals and for the stamps with which potters, leather workers, and papermakers imprint their work. It may also be as complex as a completely modeled coat of arms, with minutely detailed parts carved to several levels and internal shapes.

The most difficult part of multi-level intaglio carving is first visualizing which sections must be carved deeper than others. There are two useful aids. A small model of wax, plastelene, clay, or even bread (see page 59) is a handy relief or reverse reference, and it need not be at full scale or even completely detailed to be very useful. Moistened, kneaded bread pressed into the carving as you progress gives a quick relief check of the intaglio design. Clay, wax, or plastelene also work but tend to stick to or stain some varieties of wood.

LOW-RELIEF CARVING

The next logical step following incised carving is *low-relief carving.* In its simplest form, it is simply incised carving with the background cut away. The black-line woodcut (see page 43) is a simple relief.

Good practice for carving simple relief are the geometric or stylized patterns often used in repeated forms around frame and shelf edges or anywhere a

LOW RELIEF CARVING on this panel has intricate, detailed design which gives deceptive depth impression.

repeat, or diaper, form of decoration is indicated. Excellent idea sources for this type of pattern are books on the stylized family crests used in Japan, and others on designs for craftsmen. Both are available in most libraries.

Excellent practice projects for more detailed multi-level-relief carving are knotted ropes, oak, maple, or acanthus leaves. The knotted rope develops your eye for elements of design that pass over and under each other.

After laying out the pattern on the surface (see below), set in the outline by making stop cuts all along the lines separating the raised design from the background areas. Rough out the background areas with as wide and quick a gouge as can comfortably be used in the area. Remember to set in and rough out in several stages if the background is to be lowered more than one-eighth inch. Wherever possible, work across the grain and toward the stop cuts, and be sure not to cut deeper than the bottom of the stop cuts or you can split past the cuts and ruin the work.

The rough-cut background may then be smoothed by use of somewhat flatter gougers, firmers, or skew firmers. (Some workers prefer to leave a strip of background unfinished immediately next to the relief design and finish it at the same time as the adjacent relief to allow for any tool slips while working the raised portions.) The degree of grounding or smoothing of the background will depend on its intended appearance. Except in the case of extremely formal medallions and commemorative carvings, the background is seldom made perfectly smooth. Tool marking of some type is usually desirable to accentuate the difference between relief and background. Texture can be produced by controlled, with-the-grain gouge marks, slice marks, cross-hatch grooving with a parting tool, toothed scrapers, or wood stamps. A grounding trick often used to accentuate shadow lines around raised designs is to use a veiner to deepen the ground around the outline. Another is to slightly undercut the design where the appearance of a thin design edge and deep shadow would be desirable. Undercutting is especially effective when the design is of such recognizable elements as leaves, which look mis-shapened if left thick-edged. If the piece is to be permanently viewed from only above or below, undercutting need only be done on the side nearest the viewer.

Bosting, or rough carving of the raised design, follows normal outlining and setting-in steps that precede all material-removal operations. Roughly shape the pattern elements, using as wide and quick a gouge as the size and shape of the design will allow. Cut to within a fraction of an inch of the final depth,

---

HOW TO LAY OUT A PATTERN

There are three easy methods for enlarging or laying out patterns. The classic method is that of grid sketching, in which a grid is first drawn or laid directly over the original pattern. A similar grid, scaled to suit the final size desired, is drawn on a sheet of paper. The places where major outlines of the original intersect lines at the overlaid grid are noted, then marked on the work grid at the same relative points. Sketching then becomes a fairly simple matter of connecting up the marked points with short sketch lines.

Probably the simplest solution for most people is to photograph the original on color slide film, then project the developed slide on a wall to which you have attached a piece of tracing paper. With this technique you have the most control over size, and even if the original is black-and-white, you can see all detail as it appeared on the original. If you do your own photo processing, you can use your enlarger in much the same way.

An overhead or opaque projector may be used to project page-size originals, but these are bulky, expensive, and hard to find.

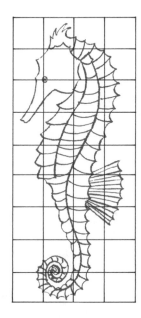

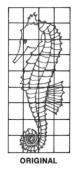

ORIGINAL

APPLY GRID TO ORIGINAL,
ENLARGE SECOND GRID
TO SIZE DESIRED,
AND SKETCH IN DESIGN

leaving just enough wood for smooth, uninterrupted final modeling cuts.

Modeling, or final shaping, should be accomplished wherever possible with single cuts for small planes or details, such as single flower petals. Single, uninterrupted cuts made with a sharp tool leave clean polished surfaces that unify the detail.

If you know where the finished piece is to be displayed and the normal direction of light under which it will be viewed, it is a good idea to check the piece during modeling by moving a lamp around to duplicate the relative angle of the final viewing light source. Without these lighting checks, relief that looks right under normal workbench light may later appear too deep or too shallow. Added advantages of checking under a movable light are familiarity you can develop with the play of light and shadow over relief, and how much actual carving may be necessary to suggest complicated detail.

HIGH RELIEF CARVING

High relief carving might be called relief carving in depth, with many of the requirements and problems of carving in-the-round. In many cases, portions can be so thoroughly modeled and undercut that they

ALEXANDER ZELLER

USE LAMP to check finished piece for areas that may appear too deep or shallow under final viewing light.

ALEXANDER ZELLER

PIERCED RELIEF is shown in detailed carving of coat of arms at cabinet top; lower portion is low relief.

seem to be totally separate from the background, but such fine carving involves reaching back between elements to undercut. This has probably been the inspiration for some of the weirdly wonderful left and right-curved and short claw-like bent tools so exciting to the acquisitive beginner. If you ever do finely detailed work of this sort, you might find that reworked dental picks are just right for many tight spots.

A close look at some of the fantastically detailed religious high reliefs of the 16th through 19th centuries quickly shows that high relief often includes several techniques: carving in-the-round on some isolated portions; high relief over the major raised portions; low relief in the partial background; both incised and intaglio carving in the actual background.

A common detail in high relief is pierced carving, in which the design goes completely through the background. This is used for screens and panels or wherever light or air must pass through. Modeling must continue over the edges of the pierced holes if a finished appearance is desired.

High relief lends itself to the realistic approach because the observer tends to expect greater detail than in low relief. Simple suggestion of shape by rounding off corners of otherwise flat surfaces isn't enough. The sides of raised portions must be detailed as well as the outer surfaces, and leaf edges left unthinned by undercutting will look heavy. Faces must look like faces, not simply boxes with features.

Grain direction becomes much more of a problem where thin elements have to be undercut and even partially freed from the background. It would be fatal, for instance, to carve a figure holding a walking stick which had to be even partially separated from the background in such a way that the grain ran across the narrow stick. The same would apply to an extended arm or leg. So plan the physically weak points of the design to fall precisely right on the grain.

Perspective becomes more of a problem on very high relief where recognizable scenes are involved. A background object must be relatively smaller than an identical object in the foreground, or the scene will appear flattened. Though we use perspective information unconsciously in everyday life for judging location, distance, and size, many of us fail to recognize it as a specific phenomenon. To develop an awareness of perspective, try framing a view by holding up a piece of cardboard with a 4 by 5-inch cutout a few inches in front of your eyes, relating the apparent positions and sizes of near versus far objects to the frame.

Don't let perspective scare you out of trying high relief. It is a great deal more difficult to write about than to do. Study perspective painlessly by examining photographs or paintings. Or, look through any of the books on perspective for amateur artists which can be found at your library or book store.

GLENN C. MC CUNE

DEPTH OF HIGH RELIEF is readily evident in this realistic carving of stampeding horses. Note that sides of figures have as much detail as outer surfaces and that background sizes are smaller than those in foreground.

LAMINATING WOOD

When properly done, wood lamination can be a life-saver if you need a large carving block, an unusual color or grain combination, or want a contrasting surface to cut through for chip, relief, or intaglio carving.

Lamination can range from adding a single layer of veneer to a solid block, through the gluing together of several large blocks of wood, to the sand-

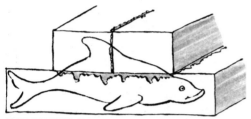

LAMINATE WOOD BLOCKS TO FIT SPECIFIC PROJECT

wiching of many sheets of plywood to produce the striated appearance often found in modern art and furniture. Plywood is, in itself, a prime example of lamination.

When many thin striations are desired, you can start with fitches of veneer, but plywood greatly simplifies and lessens the work. You may want to use special veneers between sheets of plywood for specific color combinations not normally attainable through the use of plywood alone.

Lamination of larger wood blocks requires a little more planning. Direction and pattern of grain will be readily visible in the finished piece, may affect workability, and the blocks may have to be inserted in specific directions for strength or appearance. Thin sections of the finished piece—such as a leg or arm —should have grain running vertically for maximum strength.

Liquid white glues are adequate for gluing smaller pieces intended for use indoors. Avoid them on pieces that will be exposed to heavy shear forces at joints, high temperatures, high humidity, or moisture. Liquid white glues develop a glacier-like creep under heavy shear forces and heat, and seriously weaken under high humidity or moisture.

Plastic-resin glues—light-brown powders to be mixed with water—are probably the most useful for general wood-gluing. They provide high strength, leave light-colored glue-lines, have long shelf life when kept as dry powders, and are reasonably resistant to moisture and humidity. They are not waterproof and should not be used outdoors unless well protected by a finish coat or good shelter.

Casein glue, a creamy powder to be mixed with water, is not as readily available as the plastic-resin glue powders and is less moisture proof. But it has high strength and will readily glue oily woods such as teak and lignum vitae. This oily-wood superiority of

casein glue can be largely overcome if you must use other glues, by washing the surfaces with denatured alcohol, acetone, or lacquer thinner before gluing.

Waterproof or marine glues should be used for all outdoor work. They are usually two-component resorcinal or epoxy resins. The resorcinal resins leave a dark glue-line. Epoxies are available both clear and colored, also in putty-like consistencies for filling in poorly-fitting joints. Remember though, the thicker the glue-line, the tougher it is on knives and chisels.

Cabinetmakers' hot hide glues are extremely handy because of their quick-grabbing characteristics, which lessens the need for clamping. They are not recommended for finished pieces which will be exposed to the weather, moisture, or heat.

The popular hot-melt glues applied by electric glue guns are excellent for temporary tack-gluing or holding but are too heat sensitive for permanent work, produce too thick a glue-line, and harden so fast that only small areas can be glued at one time. For temporary glue-joints that can be released by gentle heat from an infra-red heat lamp—or simply by peeling off—they are hard to beat. An example of a temporary joint would be a carving block attached to a sheet of plywood, for clamping or for turning on a lathe against a face-plate.

Gluing pieces should be machined or planed smooth and flat to provide good surface-to-surface contact. This is preferable to a sanded surface for most glues, since wood pores and fibers are clean-cut when planed and permit maximum glue penetration. Sanded surfaces tend to become partially dust-filled and cut down glue penetration.

Mix glue to the consistency recommended by the manufacturer. If you suspect the presence of wax or oils in the wood, scrub the surfaces with denatured alcohol (shellac solvent), acetone, or lacquer thinner. Dry thoroughly before gluing.

Apply glue with an inexpensive paint brush. The amount is a matter of choice. Cabinetmakers prefer to apply the least amount that will do the job, since little is then available to squeeze out and complicate finishing and cleanup. But many carvers prefer to apply an excess to ensure maximum bonding, and depend on the fact that any squeeze-out will be removed in initial rough-shaping.

Standard woodworkers' pipe, bar, and parallel clamps can be used for many laminating situations.

By the way, keep an eye out for warped hardwood boards and warped ¾-inch plywood. They make handy extensions for clamping across wide spans. By placing them convex-side down (like rocking chair rockers), then using C-, bar, or pipe clamps to draw the raised edges down to the laminates, equal pressure is applied to the center as well as the edges of the work.

Chip-carved Trivet or Medallion

This boxwood decorative medallion or trivet is an ideal gift for any occasion. In whole or in part, the ornamental design can be adapted to innumerable items; the diaper patterns on the outer edges of front or back could be used for jewelry and buttons, door handles and panels, for rosettes at shelf corners, or in strip form on shelf edges or frames. The central portions of front and back would make excellent panel designs.

If the piece is to be used as a trivet—or otherwise subjected to heavy wear—use boxwood (hard to find and hard to carve), birch, beech, maple, or other tough wood. Under a clear, natural finish, light-colored woods will show up chip carving better than darker ones. Whatever the intended use, select a close-grained wood so that open pores will not interfere with the crisply carved effect desired.

Lay out and form the basic round outlines of the surrounding diaper patterns. Next, work the center floral pattern. The ten outer petals are simply twin basic triangles with A at the point of the petal, B at the center, and C at the side of the petal; the line AC is the curve.

The inner set of petals are formed from two compound triangles, with the innermost walls (the outline of the flat center section) cut as verticals.

Between adjacent petal tips and the diaper patterns are squares within squares. The smaller squares are outlined first with striking cuts, then the larger squares are cut as four-part compound triangles truncated by the small central squares.

Diaper patterns require use of most of the cuts discussed on pages 14-15 and 18-19.

The reverse side of the trivet involves a combination of chip, relief, and incised carving techniques; it may be cut almost entirely with chip carving tools plus the use of a shallow gouge for the floral element surfaces.

A clear, penetrating resin finish works well for this type of project since it has no tendency to build up in crevices and obscure the crisp cuts.

ALEXANDER ZELLER

PRACTICE CARVING floral, diaper patterns of trivet front on softwood; for finished pieces, use hardwood.

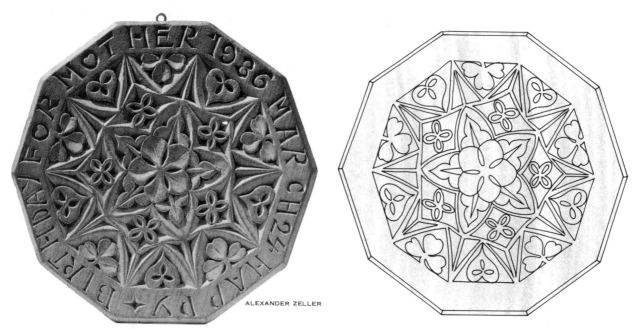

ALEXANDER ZELLER

BACK VIEW has lettering on outside rim; it can be left plain (see diagram) or carved with diaper design.

Small Cheese Tray

This project represents a transition between chip and relief carving, and may be carved in any wood suitable for food handling. The original is in mahogany.

The decorated side is made up of essentially five elements: the eight-pointed star in the center, the diamond-patterned chain around the star, the square corner rosettes, the grape-and-leaf borders, and the shamrocks between the square border and circular chain. Each element can be used separately for other projects. The grapes are often used for frames or shelf edges; the other elements for handles, jewelry, furniture, and panels. The shamrock element is used on the recessed side and is actually a repeat of the inner square on the decorated side (see drawing), but with a recess replacing the chip carving.

Hollow out and finish the tray recess, then do the shamrock corner insets.

The chip carving uses standard techniques (see pages 31-33). When working the relief portions of the border and shamrocks, remember that gouges of appropriate sweep are excellent for outlining and working curved edges. On domed or tubular shapes, the gouge may be used upside down—that is, with the concave face down—for shaping and trimming curved top surfaces.

This tray may be finished with any food-resistant finish.

ALEXANDER ZELLER

Incised Knife Holder

Based on an antique peasant design in pine, this knife holder is finished accordingly in heavy paint-based glazes.

The knife holder is a simple box made of pine. Dimensions will vary to fit the specific knives you have on hand. The incised design may be cut either before or after assembly of the box-like holder. However, the hanging handle on the assembled piece makes it easier to clamp down the extra unit for carving. Within reason, any inaccuracies of line in cutting, assembly, and carving merely add to the rustic, peasant impression. This is a good project for freehand sketching and carving.

Incise the outlines of the design and the framing line fairly deeply (⅛-inch), and make the star inside the flower from five half-lip shapes (page 33), cutting deepest at the center and surfacing at the ends.

The original has intense, house paint colors for the heart and floral elements. The background within the framing line is a pale wood tone and flat white paint is used on the frame and holder body. Bright colors were allowed to dry thoroughly. The wood tone and white areas were wiped off partially before completely dry, to reveal the wood beneath and produce a worn appearance. If your piece is to be used where water and cooking-fat vapors may accumulate, a protective, clear, synthetic top coat may be used, then rubbed back to a flat appearance with steel wool.

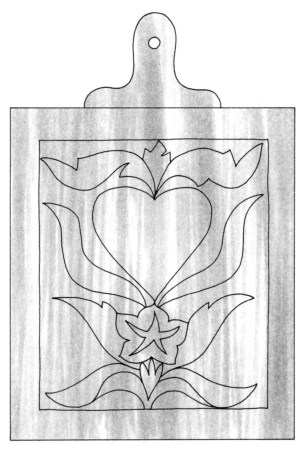

ALEXANDER ZELLER

FREE-HAND DESIGN adds to the rustic appearance of knife holder; could be used to make matching cutting board. Outline and frame the design with incised cuts ⅛-inch deep; paint with bright colors.

Woodcut

Woodcuts are simply incised carvings with the incised lines serving to outline and detail shapes. In this case the background was not reduced completely below surface level, but tool-marked with quick-gouges to leave ridges which would print as waves and clouds.

Examination of the woodcut and print quickly show that the goal is to produce the *effect* of boats, people, and structures—not accurate detailing. For example, the horizontal siding on the buildings is suggested by probably less than half the horizontal lines actually present.

Since the wave and cloud ridges are left to support the printing paper over the background areas, this woodcut can be made fairly shallow. If the background were to be entirely clear of print, it would have to be cut ¼-inch deep or more. The entire depth would allow for any paper that might sag into the cut-out areas and become soiled.

The original was cut in a piece of ponderosa pine shelving, which is satisfactory for hand-printing 50 to 100 copies. To make several hundred copies—especially if a press is to be used—use a harder wood such as cherry or birch. For special effects, woods of distinctive grain may be used. (Linoleum blocks are excellent for design practice.)

Outline the basic shapes with stop-cuts and run narrow, incised lines around the outlines. For shallow woodcuts such as this one, experienced workers often use a parting tool to incise and stop-cut in one operation, but the beginner will do well to stop-cut first.

Detailing can be done with knives, parting tools, firmers, skews, or extremely small quick-gouges designed for woodcuts and engravings. Knives, firmers, and skews are used to make narrow lip or V-cuts, or half-lip cuts (page 33). Parting tools and gouges are used to make fine running cuts. Cut a patterned or clear background with a large gouge.

Without doubt you will occasionally chip out a piece of wood where it should have stayed. Don't panic—use white glue to replace it, let it dry, and keep carving. It is a good idea to peel off any excess glue and then very lightly sand the glued surface before inking to print. Otherwise there will be a telltale difference in ink density at the repair point.

Apply printer's ink to the carved surface with a brayer (a roller made of gelatin, rubber, or plastic—you can get one at an art supply store). Carefully lay a sheet of unglazed paper (rice paper, newsprint, or papers specially designed for block printing and sold through art stores) on the inked surface. Gently but firmly rub the paper into firm contact with the raised, inked surfaces using a commercial burnisher or the bowl of a large wooden or metal spoon. Then peel the paper off the block.

PRINT (above) was made by rolling printer's ink over surface of incised woodcut (left), then pressing unglazed paper onto the inked surface. When not being used for printing, the woodcut can be displayed as wall plaque.

JOSEPH SENEY

Style Sampler for Lettering

In theory, lettering layout can be as simple as one-two-three. That is, the lower-case letters of the alphabet can be thought of as falling into three space categories. Those occupying only a single space are i, j, and l; m and w require three spaces each and all the rest occupy two. Each space is a vertical half of a square—a rectangle two units tall, one unit wide. Between-letter spacing is generally scant, but may be as much as a full single-space, depending on complexity of letter style. Single-spaces are used for punctuation marks, two spaces are left between words, and three spaces follow the punctuation mark at the end of a sentence.

Upper-case letters complicate matters a little. W and V may overlap A's so that slanted verticals parallel. The letters L and T may overlap adjoining curved letters, or each other. Because of their curved sides, D, O, P, and Q must often be brought closer to an adjoining letter to prevent a gapped appearance. In fact, two O's are often intertwined or connected to preserve the look of a solid line.

Any of the accompanying lettering styles can be "blown up" by the techniques suggested on page 36, as can any other style you may come across in art or printing texts. Newspaper advertisements are a good source of unusual lettering styles.

There are five basic carving methods for lettering: stamped, incised, intaglio, relief, and in-the-round. The basic forms of each are shown in the photograph at right. Master these, and you will be able to handle any of the fancier versions you encounter.

Stamped lettering is really more a form of texturing than carving, and is performed with any tool that will leave an impression in a wood surface when held in contact with that surface and struck with a mallet or hammer. Leatherworkers' stamping-dies are often used, or custom stamps can be made as described on page 17. The stamping can be done in the background spaces with the letter left smooth; or vice-versa, leaving the background smooth and the letter stamp-marked.

The wooden wall plaque shown below is an almost foolproof method of incised lettering. It looks good, shows obvious work, yet is very forgiving of imperfect technique. It is basically the method explained under incised carving (pages 33-34), but it is dressed up by cutting down from the outer edges toward the bottom (or centerline) with a veiner instead of attempting a smooth parallel sidewall cut with a parting tool.

It is almost always best to use the simplest lettering style appropriate to the subject (see samples on the opposite page). The simpler styles are usually easier to layout and carve and are far easier to read.

WALL PLAQUE has incised lettering. Letter style ranges from simple to complex and can be carved five ways.

ROUGH PRACTICE BLOCKS show five basic carving styles: stamped (top left), incised (top right), in-the-round (center), intaglio (bottom left), and relief (bottom right).

Optima Semi-Bold

ABCDEFGHIJKLMNOPQRSTUVWXYZ&
abcdefghijklmnopqrstuvwxyz $1234567890

Commercial Script

ABCDEFGHIJKLMNOPQRSTUVWXYZ
abcdefghijklmnopqrstuvwxyz 1234567890

Times Roman

ABCDEFGHIJKLMNOPQRSTUVWXYZ&
abcdefghijklmnopqrstuvwxyz $1234567890

Libra

aBCDEFGhIJKLMNOPQRSTUVWXYZ&
$1234567890

Old English

𝔄𝔅ℭ𝔇𝔈𝔉𝔊𝔥𝔍𝔍𝔎𝔏𝔐𝔑𝔒𝔓𝔔𝔕𝔖𝔗𝔘𝔙𝔚𝔛𝔜𝔝
abcdefghijklmnopqrstuvwxyz 1234567890

A Portuguese Tray

This is the piece shown on the cover. It is an excellent example of several of the techniques used with incised carving.

Begin by cutting the wood roughly to shape. Remember to leave the final shaping of the outermost edge until last, to allow for possible edge damage during carving.

Turn the board back-side up, lay out the tray recess, and carve to ⅛-inch depth with a large quick gouge. Use a flatter gouge to finish the final 1/16-inch. This hollowing-out serves a useful purpose beyond merely creating a tray recess. Hollowing out the back of a heavily-carved board reduces the possibility of eventual warping or splitting caused by uneven internal stresses created during carving.

To make the crosshatch design inside the rim, use a parting tool or a firmer and cut with a sweep matching the rim curve.

The chain-patterned inner rim with the tool-marked faces is produced by first cutting small, slightly overlapping, circles with a quick gouge. Then remove the overlap to leave a series of molar-like shapes. Use the same or a slightly flatter gouge to make a pair of gouge-marks on the face of each segment. Also use the gouge to recess the top of the divider strip between the resulting chain pattern and the outer crosshatch.

Outline the floral pattern with a parting tool—or use the lip-cut technique (see page 32) with firmer and gouges. Study the photograph below and the one on the cover: Note that all leaves are *gently* modeled with shallow gouges; but the flower petals are *deeply* modeled, the depth increasing toward their bases. Flower centers are left to rise back up to the surface as crosshatched pincushion or pineapple shapes.

Whenever possible, execute the final surfaces on flowers and leaves using continuous cuts. This will leave a crisp, tool-burnished effect.

Tool-mark the background with a sharp gouge, being certain to produce a clean, crisp cut both entering and leaving the wood. A dull tool will leave a rough, unattractive surface.

Use a firmer to notch the corners of the octagon and to taper the outer edges.

The original was finished with an antique brown glaze. If you prefer to retain some of the natural wood color and grain, use a base coat of semi-gloss lacquer or varnish, then apply a dark-brown glaze and wipe down.

ALEXANDER ZELLER

FLORAL PATTERN is outlined with deep incised cuts. Petals and leaves are gently modeled. Use a sharp gouge to tool-mark the background being careful to make clean crisp cuts. Finishing may show need for added carving.

Ornate Spanish Tray

Although similar to the Portuguese tray, this one is more complicated to carve, featuring more relief through undercutting of the overlapping edges.

The original was made from 1-inch white pine and stained in natural floral colors. The floral design could just as well be in colored glazes, or in gilding over gesso. If the finish is to be over gesso, any carvable wood may be used. But if clear stain and finish is intended, virtually featureless woods such as pine or basswood will be less likely to intrude on the design.

Cut the board to shape, then lay out and hollow out the back as for the Portuguese tray. Lay out the front—or top side—and cut the rim grooves with a parting tool. The wider portions can be produced simply by tilting the tool for the final cuts. Notice that the outer edge of the background is scalloped by using a quick-gouge.

Incising of the floral design is worked the same way as in the Portuguese tray, except that the background is dished *below* the floral elements at the center and left *level* at the design edges. Also, wherever elements overlap each other or stand above the background, they are undercut to give a thinner-edged effect.

Notice that even though the central stems and leaves stand above the background they are still outlined by incised lines; also note that two leaves are gouge-modeled, then incised to give the effect of veins.

CARVE BACKGROUND deeper at tray's center than at edge.

ALEXANDER ZELLER

MADE OF WHITE PINE, tray was stained in natural floral colors. Painting may require a gesso base.

ARNIE GARBORG

INCISING OF DOOR PANELS is done in same way as tray at left. Intaglio carving at top requires practice.

Poinsettia Panel

This decorative panel, with stamped background and carved frame, offers practice in four sizes and three shapes of petal elements; from the pointed outer petals to the stubby pine cone petal shapes in the center.

In spite of their apparent simplicity, the large petals present the novice with a slight problem in patience. Obtaining smooth uninterrupted surfaces like these with a minimum of tool-marking takes a lot of patience. Theoretically each petal could be formed with two cuts by a relatively flat gouge, but that also takes patience in the form of considerable practice. Sanding or riffling of the petal surfaces is a possibility, but has a tendency to deaden the living tissue appearance.

The background was carved slightly below relief level, then stamped with the joint of a ten-penny nail. Any other stamp pattern that suits your taste could be used. Start by stamping the outline of an area tight up against the relief, then work toward the center of the area.

The original—in pine—was given a mild overall brown stain which penetrated more deeply in the stamped areas, producing a darker background.

CARVE BACKGROUND of panel slightly below relief level.

ALEXANDER ZELLER

STAMPED BACKGROUND of decorative panel was made with ten-penny nail. Each panel is formed with two cuts.

ELFREDA ZELLER

SIMILAR FLORAL DESIGN can be carved with incised and chip techniques; smooth surface has minimum tool marks.

Rose Wall Plaque

Although designed as a wall plaque about 20 inches tall, this piece could have been carved larger or smaller as an applique for a door, chest, or drawer medallion. In miniature—either as is, or mounted on a wood or metal background—it would make an interesting pendant, pin, or hair ornament.

Pierced work such as this requires additional care during carving to keep from breaking any of the slender joining elements. It is a good idea to complete as much of the piece as possible before piercing and working the interior portions.

Undercut leaf and petal edges to keep them from looking as heavy as the stems. Also undercut or round-under the stems where they cross over other elements, to emphasize their round cross sections.

Texture on the original plaque was very finely tool-marked to give the faintly quilted look of living plant tissue. Yours could be given a partially or wholly polished finish, depending on intended use. The finish used on the original was natural. For jewelry use it might be interesting to color, glaze, or gild part or all of the design.

DIAGRAM can be traced, then enlarged to desired size.

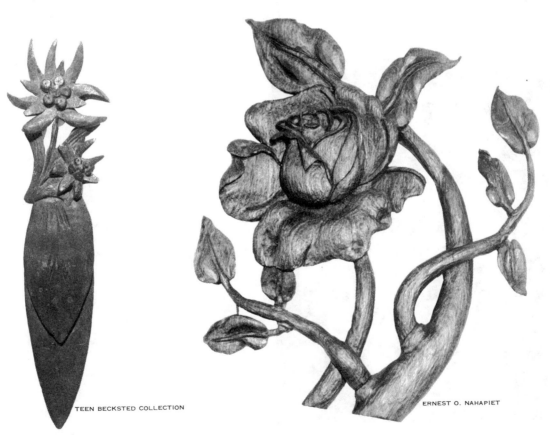

TEEN BECKSTED COLLECTION

ERNEST O. NAHAPIET

ANTIQUE LETTER OPENER, bookmark was carved from linden wood, has stained finish.

FINISHED PLAQUE can be hung on wall or attached to door as decorative panel. Same carving done in miniature can be worn as unusual pin.

Coat of Arms

Rare is the woodcarver who doesn't get the urge to carve the family crest or coat of arms—or else is asked to do one for someone else. If an example of the particular armorial bearing is not readily at hand, go to the library and refer to the several books on heraldry and coats of arms. Either make an exact copy or simplify those elements that appear too detailed.

It is the wealth of detail that make most crests appear difficult. They are usually carved as high-relief and many are pierced. Undercutting is desirable on normally thin elements such as flowers, leaves, and wings. The basic crest is often embellished with scroll work above and to the sides, as in the Winged Spur crest shown embellished in the Spanish style.

If the piece is to be used out of doors, carve it of a weather-resistant wood such as oak, cedar, or redwood. Crests or arms to be painted or gilded over a gesso base may be of any suitable wood—color and grain will be hidden. Those to be finished natural, or stained under penetrating or clear surface finishes, are most often made of mahogany, walnut, oak, teak, or other prestige wood. It might be well to consider using the traditional wood of the country of origin.

ROSEMARY NASTICH

WINGED SPUR can be carved separately for simple crest.

HENRY SOULSBY

INTRICATE DESIGN of another coat of arms was carved from oak piece using techniques given in this chapter.

OUTLINED DIAGRAM of coat of arms (above) without background can be used to make pierced relief plaque.

A Proud Chief

In spite of the apparently complicated detail, the feathered headdress consists largely of straight-line cuts and provides excellent parting tool practice.

A 2 by 12-inch piece of pine was used for this panel. It could be laminated from two or more pieces of 1 by 12-inch pine shelving.

Carve the face first to get it right before taking the time to do the surrounding detail (if you feel that you will have trouble producing the face, try modeling it from plastecine first, or carve the face alone on a scrap piece for practice). The tip of the nose is level with the frame surface. The skin texture can be obtained by meticulous gouge work to produce a smooth skin-textured surface with a minimum of obvious tool-marks. The bells and beads can be shaped by conventional gouge techniques or by inverting the gouge (concave side to work) to form smooth, curved surfaces. The stylized Indian patterns at the base are carved in relief, then the designs and background textured with parting tool and wood stamps.

Colored glazes or paints may be used: soft tones for skin and clothes, white for the feathers, and bright colors for the beads and beadwork.

ALEXANDER ZELLER

PRACTICE RELIEF CARVING of face on scrap wood or mold it in plastecine before attempting this project.

USE GOUGE to shape rounded bells, beads; Indian patterns at base can have tool-marked or stamped background.

ALEXANDER ZELLER

ZUNI INDIAN DESIGN was made using similar carving techniques; background was accented with tool marks.

Spanish Table

Built entirely of 2-inch Philippine "mahogany", this 4-foot coffee table is simply a miniature of an 8-foot dining table made for use in the same household, the only essential differences being the dimensions. You may use any dimensions you choose to fit the table into a specific space or use.

All joints are simply doweled butt joints with cut-and-fit, quarter-round molding as collars. Choose molding that matches the wood you use.

For simplicity, carve all pieces before assembly. When drilling for dowels, remember that you may not have the full wood thickness if there is carving on the opposite side. There are seven carved sections: the two end supports, the four grotesque faces carved on only one side, and the center board or spreader carved on both sides.

Spanish designs are most often built around mirror images and repeats. They are probably the most forgiving of inexact draftsmanship, layout, and carving, and often look better if the repeated patterns have slight differences in shape or detail. The low-relief designs on the supports and centerboard may be set into the surface with the background dished out for an inch or two all around the design; or the background may be flattened out to a carved frame edge. If you choose the frame edge pattern and still intend to use the half-rounds at the butt joints, be sure to allow for the portions covered by the half-rounds.

The original was carved almost entirely with skew, gouges, and mallet, with only fine detailing and clean-up done freehand. The finish was a dark-opaque, black-brown with the relief "leaded" in the traditional Spanish manner. The leading effect is accomplished by rubbing a white lead and varnish or white lead and linseed oil mixture over the relief, then rubbing it off the raised portions so that a white glaze remains in the recesses.

For a more modern version, a lighter finish could be used and a dark glaze applied to the relief and rubbed down.

BRACE AND LEG DESIGN was made up of combinations of same elements; repeated patterns may vary in detail.

ROSEMARY NASTICH

TABLE DIMENSIONS may be scaled to fit specific needs. Carving of design can be done with gouges and mallet.

Spanish Headboard

Carved of edge-doweled and glued Philippine mahogany, this headboard illustrates the use of repeated patterns, a practice common in the Spanish heritage. Each major element is carved back into the surface and visually separated from the background by broadly-dished incised outlines. The overall effect is oddly like quilting and gives a rich effect with minimal relief. To emphasize the quilt-like effect, remove any tool-marks from the background and the major top surfaces of the patterns by using rifflers and then sanding. Tool-marks may be retained in local depressions within the patterns.

Finish natural, or stain dark or blackish-brown under penetrating resins, semi-gloss lacquer, or synthetic varnish. The relief may be emphasized by "leading" (see project on opposite page) or glazing (see pages 78-79). The glaze is worked into the recesses and then wiped down, leaving just enough to bring out the detail.

CLOSEUP OF DESIGN shows four identical images.

ROSEMARY NASTICH

QUILTED EFFECT is achieved by subduing tool marked background, finish may be neutral or darkly stained.

ROSEMARY NASTICH

SPANISH BENCH has similar floral patterns on back, brace.

ROSEMARY NASTICH

CABINET DOOR designs are applicable to headboards.

A Carved Door

Virtually every design shown in this book can be adapted for decorative use on exterior, interior, or cupboard doors. The individual panels may be carved directly into the door surface as shown here, or carved separately and then either inset or attached to the surface.

Most cabinet shops can supply solid doors sized to your specifications; but insist on the best kiln-dried materials, waterproof glues, and doweled or splined construction. Remember that most solid doors are quite heavy and require two men to move them without risking damage. So even if you are in a hurry, don't take a chance on trying to lift a hefty door on or off the workbench by yourself. An efficient arrangement for working large doors is to first build a pair of waist-high saw horses, pad the tops with old toweling or carpet, then lay the door across them for convenient carving.

If the projected carving is expected to penetrate deeper than a quarter of the door thickness, make a layout so that dowels or splines can be located in such a way as to avoid the deep cuts which might expose them. Lay out your pattern, making allowance for hinge, knob, and lockset locations—especially if large antique styles are used. Notice that the lockset and knob shown are located in a plain inset set into a corner of one of the repeated patterns.

Stop-cut the outlines, rough out the background, and bost the designs (see page 36) with chisels and mallet. Complete the modeling and surfacing using gouges freehand. Tool marks on the designs themselves should be crisp-edged for maximum definition. On the background, the tool-marked edges should be softened so that they will blend into a gentle overall texture.

The original door was of Philippine "mahogany," finished a deep black-brown. This particular pattern may be emphasized by glazing or leading, but place the door in position before deciding whether or not to lead the design. On large doors the play of light and shadow is usually enough; glazing or leading may well look too "busy" or prominent.

ROSEMARY NASTICH

INDIVIDUAL PANELS are carved directly on door surface. Relief design should be crisply carved for definition.

A Small Sea Chest

Few things are as welcome in a boy's room as a sea chest in which he can store his valuables. This one was made of 1 x 12-inch pine and assembled with simple butt and miter joints. If mitering (cutting at a 45° angle) poses a problem for you, the vertical corners can be butt-jointed with the front and back panels overlapping the sides. The front and back panels may be carved prior to assembly but *after* being cut to size.

Lay out the ship pattern for the top, then stop-cut the ship, fish, and gulls. You may find it easier to get the feel of the relief levels if you begin with the frame of fish before starting on the ship—which is recessed even farther back into the wood to give the illusion of depth. The surfaces of the fish are essentially at the original surface, but the ship's sails should be *below* the original surface for best visual effect.

Notice that while both sea and sky are tool-marked, the sea is worked with short, relatively deep cuts made with a quick-gouge, while the tool marks on the sky are softened by using a flatter gouge. Also notice the use of a quick-gouge to texture the walls of the shield-like outline around the fish in the manner shown in the project on page 44.

For maximum effect the fish and the ship sails should be undercut to provide an impression of thinness. If, however, the chest is expected to serve as a seat or storage surface, undercutting will weaken the design edges and result in chipping under such use.

Lay out the front panel and work the rope frame and eagle, planning either a softly tool-marked or smooth background for the eagle. The rope frame can be simply a smooth twist, or it can be textured to give the appearance of hempen ship's line.

THOMAS R. PARKS

SIDE VIEW. Rope frame may be textured or smooth surfaced; cuts for eagle design should be crisply edged.

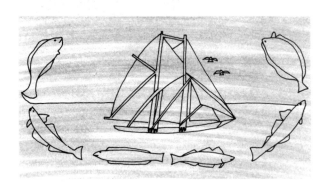

THOMAS R. PARKS

TOP VIEW. Carve background to the stop cuts of ship, fish, and gulls. Sea and sky are tool-marked with gouges.

Whittling & Carving in-the-Round

A

C

D

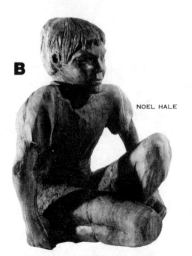

B

You can make any of the figurines shown in
A, **B**, **D**, and **E** by following the instructions for
carving in-the-round on the following pages.
Specific instructions for Boar **C** are on page 68.

Most beginning woodcarvers find it easier to carve in low-relief before approaching carving in-the-round. Shallow cutting makes it seem easier to trim the cut edges to produce an impression of form. If you have tried the several relief techniques (see pages 35-36), you will have noticed that the deeper the relief the more care and understanding of form is needed. This is why some woodworkers are hesitant to go on to carving in-the-round.

Many people have trouble visualizing the three-dimensional aspect of a carving as they work on it. The rounding between frontal plane and side plane also seems to be a problem for the beginner in realistic wood sculpture. A novice carver is apt to produce a human head resembling a rounded-off cube, with eyes, nose, and mouth on the frontal plane, and ears on two flat side planes. This effect may be admired by the cubist but is neither flattering to the

model nor satisfying to the carver attempting a realistic sculpture. Oddly enough, most carvers can recognize the problem as it develops but are reluctant to round off the corners without guidelines. If you find yourself in this spot, put down your tools, pick up some modeling clay, wax, or other moldable material, and make a scale model. Since these materials can be so easily built up or cut back, the fear of removing too much material— a real problem in woodcarving—is relieved (see page 59).

The best way to get started in carving in-the-round is to copy a good piece of sculpture. The original may be of any material. Terra cotta, plaster, and metal figurines are widely available and are useful as confidence builders, since you can carve by comparison and measurement. A few carvings made in this way will help build up your confidence and train your sense of proportion and technique. Just remember that any attempt to make an exact copy in wood of a sculpture made of another material is unwise, because the grain of your wood will often obscure fine detail (readily seen in the original) or dictate changes to take advantage of—or avoid—certain grain patterns. Also, you will probably see details of facial expression, position, or clothing that you feel you can improve on, thereby making the piece uniquely yours. Once you have finished such a piece, observe the ethics of the art—if you inscribe it, say, "A Copy of _____," then add your name after the original sculptor's.

WHITTLING AS SCULPTURE

A carver who fears the initial step into carving in-the-round would do well to start with whittling. For most people, whittling provides a great feeling of freedom from the rules and restrictions of formal carving. The pieces are usually small, and the knife cuts themselves can form the final surface, eliminating tedious

ALEXANDER ZELLER

FOUR STAGES in carving a simple figure illustrates that only basic outlines are necessary for removing waste material. Note that the hands and book were carved separately for added strength.

finishing. Fine detailing is neither necessary nor desirable on many such projects.

The combination of the words "whittled" and "sculpture" is deliberate, to emphasize the fact that whittling is no less true sculpture than Rodin's *Thinker.* The difference is primarily in the scale, material, and tools. Usually, the whittler's figures are small, and he confines himself to wood as the material and knives as the tools.

Whittling acquired a poor reputation at the hands of the old-time, store-front "stick-wasters," who sat by the hour *just a-whittl'n*, judging their individual ability solely by the size of the pile of chips produced. Time and the works and writings of master whittlers have largely remolded the old image, and whittling is now recognized as a valid art form.

Whittling in-the-round is the type most commonly done, but with the help of a canoe knife (the whittler's gouge—see page 17) and other special blades, *any* relief carving can be accomplished by whittling. Knives and other whittling blades have enjoyed a significant return to favor among woodcarvers in recent years.

Soft, non-resinous woods such as northern white pine, basswood, poplar, cottonwood, cedar, and redwood are usually used. It is wise to start with one of these, simply because they are relatively easy to cut and control, reasonably priced, and generally available. After a little experience, almost any carvable wood can be used, even lignum vitae. But remember that you will be holding the wood in one hand while you whittle, so that the harder the wood, the harder

the cutting pressure and the greater the damage if you slip.

BASIC PATTERNS FOR SHAPING

Detailed patterns and drawings are seldom very useful—except as references—for in-the-round carving, since the original surfaces of the carving block are quickly removed, taking the pattern with them. Only the basic outlines of the piece need be transferred to the raw block to provide guidance for bulk removal of waste material. Obviously, you will need front, back, and side views. Position the outlines to take advantage of the best grain of the wood—take particular care to position thin, freestanding sections for maximum strength.

Besides the outlines, it is always a good idea to locate the vertical centerline of the finished piece (not the raw block) to give yourself a standard reference. Many carvers also add horizontal lines around the block at important locations (such as shoulders, hips, waist, and knees of a projected statue) as a help in visualizing proportion and location.

If you have a detailed layout, or an original to be copied, make a full-scale cardboard template to hold up to the work occasionally as a quick check on progress. A pair of calipers may be used to transfer measurements from layout to work, but this technique is generally tedious since it provides only a single point-to-point measurement with each setting. However, a detailed layout at a scale *other* than that desired for the work can be calipered if a pair of proportioned dividers are used.

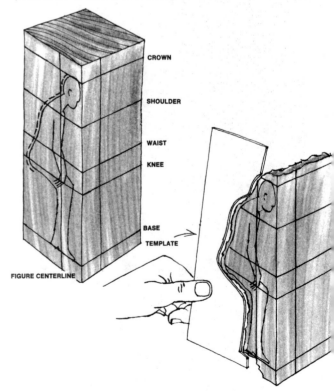

CROWN

SHOULDER

WAIST

KNEE

BASE

TEMPLATE

FIGURE CENTERLINE

USING THREE-DIMENSIONAL SKETCHES

In the planning stages of any woodcarving project, it is often very handy to have a model of the finished project that can be readily reworked or shaped to provide an approximation of the final product—a sort of three-dimensional sketch. Among the materials well suited to making three-dimensional sketches are clay, plastecine, polystyrene foam, soap, and wax.

Clay is obtainable in self-hardening form or the type that requires kiln-baking to harden. Either can be used for three-dimensional sketches. Keep the material moist while working, and wrap in plastic sheet or bags between work sessions. For long term or permanent retention, the self-hardening clays are most convenient. Work the moist clay with fingers, spatulas, spoons, wires, sticks, or any of the pre-shaped clayworking tools available at art and ceramic supply stores. Partially-dry clay can be cut with knives, chisels, or scrapers. Hard-dried or baked clay can be worked with powered burrs, stonecarver's chisels, files, rasps and rifflers, and abrasives.

Commercially available papier mâché powder, plaster of Paris, spackling compound, or wood putty can all be prepared as directed by the manufacturer, modeled and carved like moist clay until hard, and worked with woodworking tools after hardening.

Plastecine and other non-hardening modeling compounds are handled like moist clay, although water is not needed to keep them pliable.

Polystyrene foam is useful where broad shapes are to be sketched. It is lightweight and can be rapidly shaped with knives, saws, rasps, and abrasives. The open-cell structure tends to hide detail unless filled in with wood putty, spackling compound, or wax.

Soap carving provides a handy, easily-carved material for detail sketching. Knives, chisels, scrapers, nails, nail files, and wire can be used to carve soap. Repairs can be made, or pieces added, by first dipping a knife blade in hot water, then holding the hot, wet blade between the pieces to be joined until surfaces soften, after which the blade is removed and the sections clamped together until dry. Detail can be accentuated by brushing on colored shoe polish, allowing to dry, then buffing raised surfaces clean.

Wax, in its several forms, is extremely useful and, for many craftsmen, the most versatile carving medium for three-dimensional sketches. It can be softened with heat for molding to shape or for forming large blocks or sheets. When molded, it can be hardened faster than most other materials to carvable consistency. By use of a heated blade, it can be repaired, built up, or added-to at any time with a minimum of fuss. A high gloss can be given to

wax carvings by rapidly passing a clean flame over the surface. Perhaps most important to the cost-conscious, wax can be reused many times by simply melting down, and it's non-abrasive nature makes it easy on carving tools.

Candle wax, either in the form of blocks or ready-made candles, is widely available and may be used as is or remolded after adding color. In fact, multi-colored layers can be produced for dramatic effects with incised, relief, or intaglio carving similar to that obtained by carving through laminated wood surfaces. Any wood or linoleum-block carving tool can be used. Work boldly, but don't try to cut deep at each pass or the wax will chip. Gentle heating reduces this tendency to chip but can cause deformation of fine detail. Tools heated over a clean flame or hot plate may also be used, but this will require some practice to avoid overheating and damaging the tool itself, or causing bubbling and flowing in the wax. Of special interest is the forming wax sold specifically for making sculptured and hand-formed candles.

There are special waxes prepared for sculptors, dentists, and jewelers, who use them for modeling pieces to be cast in metal by the lost-wax process. These are usually more expensive and harder to find than candle waxes. They are, however, easier to handle in that they are harder and more metal-like in their toolability, will hold finer details, and have greater structural strength in thin cross sections.

A useful technique in building up shapes in wax is to start with thin sheets of wax and cut out shapes with hot wires or blades. Fuse the cut pieces together by running a clean flame over a surface to barely wet-melt it, then applying the adjoining piece. Or, you may simply stack them together and edge or spot-weld with flame or hot spatula.

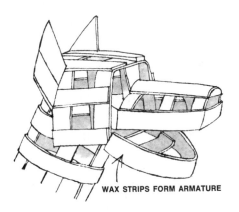

WAX STRIPS FORM ARMATURE

CUTTING THE WOOD TO ROUGH SHAPE

Large chunks of waste wood may be removed by any convenient means: handsaw, bandsaw, chain, or sabre saw; chisel, rasp, or axe. When band-sawing waste material from a block intended for carving in-the-round, either stop just short of cutting the waste section completely free (but far enough so that it can be *broken* free) or cut it free and then temporarily tack it back into place. If completely removed, it may leave an inconveniently-angled support surface for cutting away the waste on the

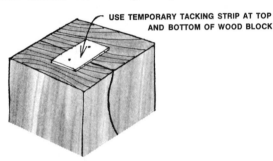

USE TEMPORARY TACKING STRIP AT TOP AND BOTTOM OF WOOD BLOCK

adjoining sides—as well as removing other layout lines.

When you begin to carve, you may find yourself gingerly slicing off whiskers of wood as though the block might suddenly yell "Stop!" Eventually, in doing highly-polished sculpture on highly-figured woods, you may learn to let the wood "speak" to you and guide your carving. This will not, of course, be the case when working with the soft, virtually figure-free woods such as northern white pine or basswood, which are the ones usually used for whittling.

Practice long, sweeping, decisive cuts when whittling. Each cut should remove the maximum amount of wood consistent with the ultimate shape desired and the workability of the wood. After becoming thoroughly familiar with large, decisive cuts, you will soon learn to adjust the length, breadth, depth, and shape of the cut to obtain the desired texture effect (see pages 14-16 for blade descriptions and knife-handling).

TEXTURING SURFACES

Experienced carvers divide sharply on the question of surface texture. Some prefer to leave the tool marks, others remove them by scraping or sanding. Don't join either group wholly—use whichever technique will produce the effect that appeals to you. At first glance, tool-marked pieces may strike you as the easiest to make, since sanding and finishing is eliminated. But once you've tried to make one, you will find that considerable thought and skill is re-

quired to create tool marks of the optimum size, shape, direction, and location to suggest the texture and detail desired.

If you decide to sand, completely remove all traces of tool marks, because partial smoothing lacks both the character of clean tool-marking and the satin smoothness expected of a sanded surface. Also defer any sanding until all knife and chisel work is complete. Abrasive particles left in the wood surface by sanding can wreak havoc with cutting edges.

Articles such as plates, bowls, spoons, and tongs should be smooth-finished on food-contacting surfaces for ease of cleaning. Outer surfaces on such items may be, and often are, left with tool marks for textured effects.

CHISEL CARVING IN-THE-ROUND

Choose and set up your block of wood so that, as nearly as possible, the grain will lie in such a way that you can work mostly from top to bottom.

Since all surfaces except the bottom will show in the finished piece, the problem of holding the work during carving arises. There are several possible solutions:

- Attach a piece of plywood to the bottom with glue or screws as a temporary base for clamping in place.
- Leave extra wood at the bottom for vice-clamping, then later remove the excess.
- Clamp directly with C or bar-clamps, hold-downs, or vices, but be careful of marring the surfaces.
- Use a woodcarver's screw through the bench top.
- Arrange sandbags as cradles to hold the work horizontally.

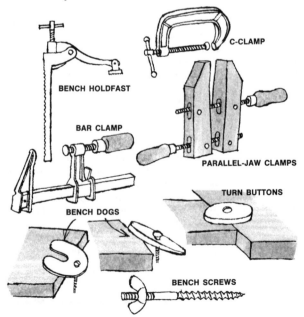

C-CLAMP

BENCH HOLDFAST

BAR CLAMP

PARALLEL-JAW CLAMPS

TURN BUTTONS

BENCH DOGS

BENCH SCREWS

If you use a sculptor's stand which you can walk around while you work all surfaces, any method that holds the work steady is satisfactory. The plywood baseboard is especially useful when you must work in front of a standard bench, since the baseboard can be held firmly with C-clamps or hold-downs yet quickly loosened to allow rotating the work for access to the sides and back. Sandbags serve to stabilize the work and protect previously-carved surfaces when either size or convenience require that the piece be held horizontally.

Layout lines will have to be re-drawn as you proceed into the block. Vertical centerlines and horizontal height-location lines also help (see page 58).

Re-read the section on handling gouges and firmers (see pages 18-19), and remember that since you are working on all sides of the block, you are liable to run into areas of apparent change in grain direction. Grain is seldom consistent throughout any plank or block. Thus, one side may offer a good downward cutting-face while its opposite side presents rough grain-ends to a downward-cutting chisel.

CARVING WITH POWER TOOLS

Powered carving tools can speed up the roughing-out and detailing of a carving or sculpture. As with any tool there are specific techniques for use, and the best work can only be done with practice. The newcomer to power-carving is well advised to go slow, operate the motor exactly at the speeds and loads specified, to make small cuts only, and progress from broadly-stated shapes to more detailed work only as practice, confidence, and experience build up.

Except for the extremely powerful grinders and routers, most powered carving tools are not likely to harm even the inexperienced (beyond a skinned knuckle or finger) simply because of their ease of handling and relatively low power. However, their high speeds enable them to remove more material than their apparent power might lead you to expect. With even reasonable care, safety is easily achieved. The higher-powered grinders and routers deserve a great deal more respect where safety is concerned, simply because they can exert enough muscle to wrench themselves out of your control if the bit becomes jammed in the work. Side-cutting, router-type bits can be particularly dangerous to the project and operator if the machine gets out of control.

All rotary-carving power tools can use burrs, drills, router bits, grinding wheels, sanding drums and disks, disk-saws, and abrasive cut-off wheels—within the size limitations of the chuck or collet, and manufacturer's specifications. Some bits, drums, or wheels may require reducing the tool speed by the solid-state motor speed control specified by the manufacturer.

For maximum utility, some method of speed control for the motor is desirable. Check the manufacturer for his specific recommendations before buying a speed control at random. Resistance-type controls tend to overheat most modern high-speed motors—though they do work on some sewing machine power units, which can be adapted to make good bench and flexible-shaft motors.

Don't grind down the ¼-inch shank of a ½-inch diameter burr to fit a ⅛-inch chuck on a light-duty grinder. You will probably burn out the motor under the excess load created by the large burr diameter.

Most large-collet chucks can be adapted to smaller tool shanks with collet adapters available from the manufacturer. Smaller-than-original equipment shanks may, however, tend to snap or twist off under the high torque of larger machines.

Maintain control at all times. Make several light cuts instead of one heavy cut and brace the arm controlling the tool or holding the workpiece against your body or workbench.

Never insert a side-cutting tool, such as a burr or router bit, into a hole the same size or slightly larger than itself. The chances are that at some point it will bounce just enough to rebound off the opposite side and produce a distinctive kick and buzzing—also a mangled carving. Try to use a bit half (two-thirds at most) the size of the space in which it will be working.

If the bit starts to smoke, turns blue-black, or gives off a smell of burnt wood, you are using either too high a motor speed or too much pressure for the specific tool and wood combination—or the tool is dull.

Too slow a speed will produce a bumping tool action which does little effective cutting and leaves a rough surface.

Grinder-type tools may be hand-held and advanced into the work, or may be bench-mounted and the work then manipulated under the tool bit. Whether the mounting is vertical or horizontal, it must be rock-steady, or the work will stutter and bounce against the tool with resulting damage to both tool and work.

Grinders with flexible shafts and speed controls are probably the easiest to control. Remember not to apply sudden heavy pressure at the bit or the shaft will break or be bent out of shape.

Always wear safety glasses, goggles, or a face shield when using a power tool. A flake of wood or metal driven by the 20,000 to 30,000 rpm of a grinder motor can make short work of an eye.

A Fancy Clothes Hook

The original is probably of German or Swiss origin. Whittled from a soft wood, it is an intriguing and useful gift for a family room, cabin, or child's room. The hook itself presents a strength problem since the vertical grain makes it somewhat weak in the center. Drill from the back, and glue in one or more wood or steel dowels as shown in the diagram.

For variations on this pattern, simply substitute the head of any of the projects shown in this book, or any others that appeal to you. Children's story book characters are especially fitting for children's rooms. As a contrast, the figure can be left with toolmarks and the hook finished smooth.

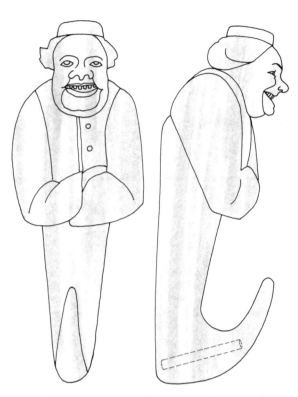

INSERT DOWEL into back of hook for added strength.

TEEN BECKSTED COLLECTION

ROUGH-OUT SHAPE following vertical, horizontal guidelines (see page 60); hardwoods are best for strength.

CARVE FACIAL and clothing details according to individual preference; finish can be smooth or tool-marked.

From a Stick of Wood – a Ball and Chain

There is a certain fascination connected with the creation of a chain from a single stick of wood. When you add a cage full of carved wooden balls to the end of the chain, it becomes a conversation piece. The original shown was made from 2 by 2-inch pine, but by reducing the size to a ¾ by ¾-inch stick, a fine key chain results.

First practice making a chain of pine or basswood. Whittling is easier with these soft woods when you have to pierce through between links. After a little practice, any of the close-grained hardwoods can be used—the harder the wood, the harder the work and the more durable the chain.

The best procedure is to start whittling at the free link end and work toward the ball and cage, so that you have a solid handle to hold while working. Complete as much of the shaping on each link as possible before freeing it from its neighbor and from the cage. Free links and balls tend to be difficult to whittle or carve on, and you might damage adjoining or connecting pieces. A fine pen blade or hobby knife with interchangeable blades is good for the final freeing operation.

Be certain that the balls protrude slightly between the bars and that the freeing cuts are narrow or the balls will tumble out of the cage.

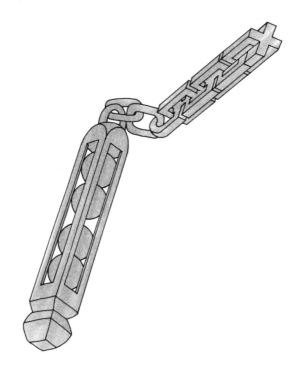

BEGIN WHITTLING at free link end, work toward handle.

JENE A. PARKER

USE CLOSE-GRAINED HARDWOODS to make strong and durable chain or letter opener (at right). Final carving of chain links to make them movable should be done with a fine pen blade or craft knife.

Timber!—or One-finger Pierre

Reminiscent of the good-natured jokester who seems to be a fixture in every small lumber camp of the north woods, this whittled scene may be made in four parts. The base is a flat piece of driftwood and the tree trunk a section of a branch; the axe and Pierre himself are of pine, though any suitable wood could be used. The separate parts are pegged together with dowels.

The base and tree trunk will depend largely on the specific natural materials available to you. Keep the chips cut from the trunk to glue to the base as shown in the photo. Pierre may be carved from a single piece of wood, but the tree-supporting hand may have to be carved separately and inset into the sleeve in order to have the grain paralleling the pointing finger. Finish Pierre's clothing with oil or acrylic paint or enamels. His face and hands may be left natural or lightly glazed to simulate a ruddy complexion.

Special care should be taken to preserve Pierre's "Look at me—I'm going to push it over!" expression.

CARVE POINTING HAND separately and inset into arm.

PAUL A. DERBY

USE PEGS to connect base and tree trunk to figure.

MARSHALL "BUD" FRACK

ROUGH FINISHES add to figures' rustic appearance.

PAUL A. DERBY

CARVE THREE FIGURES separately, mount to round base.

MARSHALL ''BUD'' FRACK

ROUGHLY FINISHED BOOKEND is attached to figure.

MARSHALL ''BUD'' FRACK

PAINT was used to accent facial and clothing details.

FRANCIS X. COOK

LACQUER FINISHED FIGURES are placed on smooth base.

A Spurtle—Handy in the Kitchen

The photograph below shows a pair of salad spoon-and-fork sets, a pierced wooden stirring paddle, and an unusual but extemely handy cooking tool called a *spurtle.* This odd gadget originated in Scotland where it was mostly used for stirring porridge. But it spread across Europe and became an all-around kitchen tool, equally valuable for stirring, lifting, pouring, and tasting. The friend who receives a spurtle as a gift may enjoy explaining it as much as using it.

More familiar are the salad sets—the smaller set is just right for at-the-table family use, while the larger is intended primarily for informal serving at the buffet. All the pieces shown are fairly easy to make, but don't go overboard on decoration. Remember that fancy carving on food-handling tools tends to collect and retain food particles, making cleaning rather difficult.

If you prefer decorative carving on the handles, almost any chip-carved, incised, relief, or in-the-round pattern shown elsewhere in this book can be adapted.

Lay out the pattern on a piece of clear hardwood such as mahogany, Philippine "mahogany," walnut, oak, ash, maple, or rosewood, On harder woods, roughing-out by saw will speed things up. Whittle the outline shape normally. The bowls of the spoon and fork may be hollowed out by canoe knife (see page 17) or by careful slicing with a spey blade. If you decide to make the bowl exceptionally deep, drilling into the waste will speed the whittling operation.

Sand all surfaces smooth. A band-sander is ideal for all but the insides of bowls. Finish with a food-resistant, oil-resistant, and acid-resistant finish, such as one of the food-vessel finishes sold at wood-craft stores.

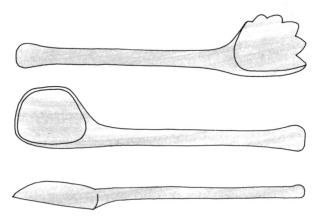

ENDS of spoon and fork are thicker for hollowing out.

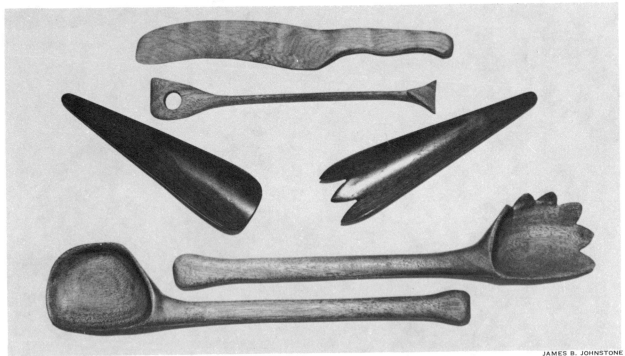

JAMES B. JOHNSTONE

UTENSILS were finished with a food, oil, and acid-resistant finish; decorative carving is optional.

Leaf Bowl

This bowl was made from Honduras mahogany, but walnut or any other wood with sufficient strength for the thin stem-spiral would be satisfactory.

Rough-shape the leaf and stem but do not pierce or thin out the stem until work on the rest of the bowl is complete. Handling during carving of the bowl could result in a broken stem-piece.

To save time in hollowing out the bowl you might consider using a drill bit or end mill to remove the bulk of the interior waste by repeating drilling. Be sure to limit the depth of your drilling to prevent breaking through the bowl bottom.

Use a large quick-gouge to shape the inside of the bowl. Make it as smooth as possible with gouges, then sand it smooth.

Shape the outside of the bowl, matching the outer and inner contours to provide a thin lip edge. Shape that portion of the stem which forms the spine of the leaf; then tool-mark the outer surface of the leaf in the pattern shown, using the appropriate narrow quick-gouge, fluter, or veiner.

The delicate part follows. Form the rough shape of the thick end of the stem—top, bottom, and sides —using a coping saw, band saw, or rasps. Pierce the areas between the stem segments, then rough-shape with gouges or knives. Most people find knives easier for this part of the project. Complete shaping with shallow gouges, then sand.

A clear, food-resistant lacquer or synthetic resin finish is indicated when the bowl is made for use as a serving dish.

ALEXANDER ZELLER

FRONT has polished surface which accents grain swirls.

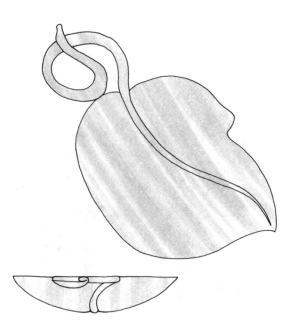

DEPTH of bowl may vary with thickness of wood.

TOOL MARKING of bottom adds texture to leaf design.

The Boar

The effect of power and animal strength in this sculpture depends on the judicious use of a deeply gouge-marked surface. The original was carved from a single block of pine.

Rough-shape by saw or chisel, but do not pierce between legs until after the body and base have been completed. Notice, from the grain of the base, that the original was carved with the grain running vertically to provide maximum strength through the legs. The two long sides of the base are finished smooth, as a counterpoint to the rough texture of the boar.

The lines between neck and foreleg and at the leading edge of the hams are slightly deeper cut, and the tool-marks overlapped to provide visual emphasis.

Avoid the temptation to center the figure on the base. Set further back than shown, it becomes static and loses that aggressive forward thrust. Don't fatten the beast to a more "porkerish" outline or it will lose the characteristic leaness of the wild.

Gouge-cutting will have to be from several directions to keep from hogging into the grain. Be especially sure to use razor-sharp gouges across the end grain on back, underside, and base.

Seal the wood before staining or you will have heavy penetration on top and underside, where end grain is exposed. A pigmented wiping stain, or glaze, would be an excellent choice here since the texture depends on the tool-marks rather than the wood grain.

FORWARD MOTION is achieved by carving figure off-center.

ANATOL ROMANOF

DISTINCT TOOLING gives texture and delineates form.

TEEN BECKSTED COLLECTION

NARROW TOOL MARKS on dog give appearance of hair.

The Bear

Much of the striking visual effect is produced by whittling this bear in correct relationship to the grain in a wood such as Scotch Pine or fir; the grains of woods like these have prominent visual and hardness differences between spring and summer wood.

Choose a section of 4 by 4-inch wood that has a definite pin-stripe appearance on the edge grain. Face the bear to the flat of the grain and make your layout. Remove the waste, then whittle the shape. This is one case where the grain will dictate how and where you cut. The harder summer wood edges will be darkened later and delineate the shape and detail. Examine the photograph carefully and you will see how the effect of detail is controlled by cutting through one or more layers.

Smooth the surface, then either char-and-brush or simply wire-brush (see page 75) to remove some of the soft spring wood in the grain. The charred finish needs no further coloring. The brushed version may need darkening of the raised summer wood. If so, ink the surface of a firm rubber block (or eraser) with printer's ink or pigmented stain and carefully rub it over the surface so that only the raised grain tops receive the stain.

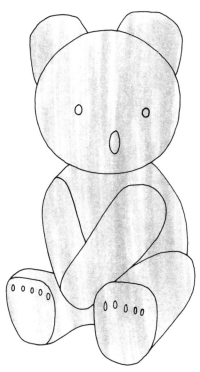

PLACE FIGURE to flat of grain when making layout.

KEVIN WARTHAN
COLLECTION

PIN-STRIPED DETAIL is supplied by wide wood grain.

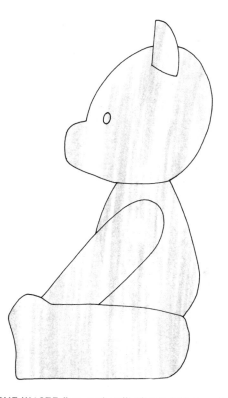

REMOVE WASTE first, grain will dictate how to cut.

Broom Handle Chess Set

A common ash broom handle was the material from which this chess set was carved. One half of the set was finished "natural" with a clear varnish, and the other half stained dark brown and varnished. Since the wood is light in color, the opposing teams could as well be stained in bright contrasting colors (ruby red and emerald green were traditional in the early history of chess).

The base pedestals may be carved either with the pieces or separately. In either case, the bases should be weighted to keep them from tipping over.

The simplest weighting procedure is to drill out the pedestal and tightly pack with "plumber's wool"— shredded lead that looks like lumpy steel wool. Melted lead is traditionally poured into the bases but this has no real advantage over the lead wool.

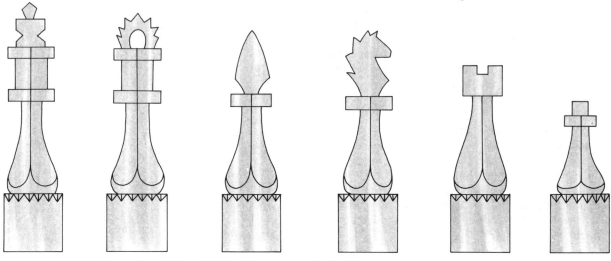

DECORATIVE DETAIL may be added to individual figures once basic shapes have been cut and smoothed.

ARTHUR RING

HALF OF SET shown here was finished natural; the other half (not shown) was stained.

Hand-carved Jewelry

Carvers who create jewelry say that besides making attractive gifts the greatest advantage of such work is that the projects are small enough to carry about in a shirt pocket, along with a knife or some miniaure tools. This great ease of portability allows carving at odd moments during the day—lunch, coffee breaks—and while riding in cars, buses, or planes.

Among the items shown here are earrings, pendants, rings, and pins. Don't neglect buttons, bracelets, necklaces, tie tacks and hair ornaments. Mechanical parts can be obtained from most hobby shops and attached by means of epoxy glue in the case of pins, tie tacks, and screw-type earring clamps; or through holes in the jewelry for fittings.

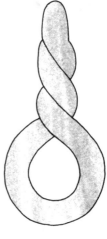

WALLACE ECK

TWISTED EARRINGS can be made from lightweight woods.

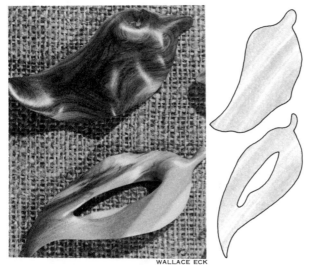

WALLACE ECK

LEAF-FORMED PINS were carved to show wood grain.

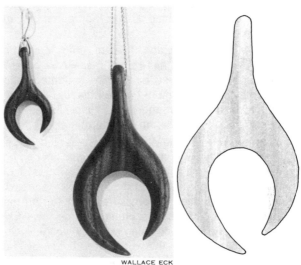

WALLACE ECK

CLAW-LIKE pendant, earring were carved from walnut.

A. M. SMITH

METAL INSERTS provide contrast to walnut finish.

GEORGE DENNINGER

IRONWOOD RING SET is accented with tiger-eye stones.

Shadow Sketches

This project is an excellent example of how an original idea can be expanded by use of imagination. The smaller unit on the left was the first one made. The tall center piece was the result of sketching the vertical shadow of the first. The horizontal piece was taken from a sketch of the shadow of the first piece when placed horizontally.

These pieces provide a good opportunity to try several techniques as a comparison of the relative ease or difficulty of rasp, chisel, and machine carving considering the comparatively simple shapes involved. For descriptive purposes, assume the left unit is chisel-carved, the center rasp-carved, and the horizontal machine-carved.

Lay out the patterns, rough out the wood with power or handsaws, then drill out the internal hole with the rasp and machine pieces. Pierce the remaining piece with gouges.

Start with the rasp piece. The entire figure can be shaped with flat and half-round rasps and coarse files. Better yet, try any one of the patented rasp tools with thin, metal multi-toothed blades; they are available in flat, half-round, and round shapes and cut very smoothly (reducing finishing time).

Whether you use the standard or patented rasps, you will quickly discover that they work best when moved at a slight angle over the work instead of being held at right angles to the surface, like a saw. You will also notice that pressure is wasted on the backstroke, as little or no cutting is done then. Except for very light finishing strokes made one-handed, always clamp the work to the bench or in a vise, and use two hands to control the tool. Finish with abrasive papers.

The chisel project should be rough-shaped with the largest quick-gouge at hand. It might be instructive to try rough-shaping one side entirely by hand-pushing the chisel and the other side using the chisel and mallet. After rough-shaping, use the size of quick-gouge that will permit working in the recesses to cut the recesses to shape. Shift to a shallower gouge, and produce as clean a final shape and finish as possible. You may want to use a firmer on parts of the front and back faces. Finish with abrasive papers. The hand strip-sander (page 79) is extremely handy for this type of project.

The machine-carved piece may be rough-carved with hand-grinders or flexible shafts with burr-type cutting bits. Note that while a few experienced machine carvers do occasionally use fluted router bits freehand for special work, these tools are extremely difficult to control and therefore dangerous in inexperienced hands. So stick to burr-type cutters. (See page 22 for instructions on use of grinders.) Produce as smooth a finish as possible with the burrs, then complete finishing with a band or flap sander, if available, or sand it by hand.

When finished, if the pieces are well done, it should be difficult to tell which section was done by which method. Any of the pieces could, of course, be done by any of the three methods.

Color or finish is largely a matter of personal choice—though in most surroundings a medium to dark tone is very effective since reflections and highlights will show up better. A penetrating-resin or semi-gloss lacquer finish will show the surface off to good advantage, but will also accentuate any nicks or bumps.

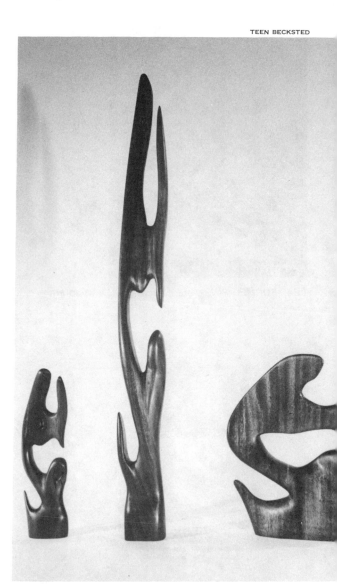

TEEN BECKSTED

CENTER FIGURE was made from shadow of figure at left.

Log Figures

First find a log big enough for the job, season for several years (see page 8), then carve. If you have a choice, pick a log that most nearly fits the shape you have in mind. If the piece is to be given a clear finish, wood grain, color, and texture will be important factors. If it is to be painted, then any durable wood may be used. The figures shown here are of redwood, which is relatively light weight and lends itself to easy handling and carving. Local additions for protruding parts of the design can be glued to the log. In this type of work it is common practice to carve arms, hands, etc., separately and then dowel them in position.

It is generally a good idea to have full-sized drawings when working larger-than-life, but simple chalk lines on a wall are adequate. Most of the rough shaping can be done with a light-weight chain saw: a gasoline model if used outdoors or away from power lines, and an electric model for indoor use. Choose a light-weight model with solid chain bars. Bars with nose wheels tend to be troublesome when the nose of the chain bar is used for hollowing operations. Gasoline models are noisy, but dependable and free of the entangling power line which can be a problem on large projects. If you use an electric chain saw, choose only the heaviest-duty model available; the inexpensive "homeowners" electric saw may not hold up under the heavy use of carving.

Electric grinders (heavy-duty) may be useful for shaping, but the *fastest* shaping and modeling can be done using a sculptor's adze, or with chisels and mallet.

Surface textures can range from rough saw-cuts through tool-marking to glassy smooth. Too smooth a painted finish tends to make it look as though it were cast of metal, plaster, or plastic. Natural-finish abstracts can look extremely good when given a highly polished surface, either in part or overall.

Occasional cracking and splitting is inevitable in log-carving, but such defects do not necessarily make a carving unacceptable. If cracks or splits *must* be patched, putties or fillers that will compress or crumble under pressure are preferable since aging, temperature variation, or humidity changes may cause a crack to narrow spontaneously. Hard fillers or wood inserts can resist closing up of the crack and promote further splitting.

For interior display almost any finish may be used. For prolonged exposure to sun and weather, pick paints and clear finishes specifically designed for severe exterior use. To be really sure, write directly to the paint manufacturer.

MARSHALL "BUD" FRACK

LARGE LOGS and generous workspace are needed to make these figures; full-sized drawings are also helpful.

Finishing Techniques

ANATOL ROMANOF

A

MARSHALL ''BUD'' FRACK

C

PAUL A.
DERBY

B

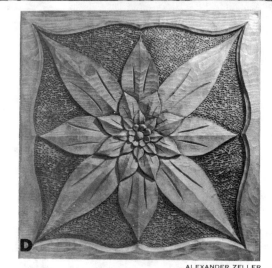

ALEXANDER ZELLER

D

Finishes on these examples are—**A**: Tool-marked.
B: Matt. **C**: Paint. **D**: Stamped. **E**: Lacquer.

*O*n any piece of tooled wood where a finished, permanent appearance is desired, the *basic* techniques of wood furniture-finishing apply. There are, however, several finishes seldom used on furniture which are appropriate for carvings.

SPECIAL TEXTURING EFFECTS

Whatever the nature of the carving, striking effects can be obtained by processes that depend on further development of the wood surface before application of a protective finish.

Burnishing is a method of producing a sheen on the wood by rubbing with a hard object such as wood, bone, or glass—or alternatively with a fistful of excelsior or shavings. Rubbed with a solid object, the wood develops beautiful, polished highlights. To obtain an overall sheen on a tool-marked surface, use the excelsior or shavings. Steady, hard pressure is required as you rub. The softer the rubbing material

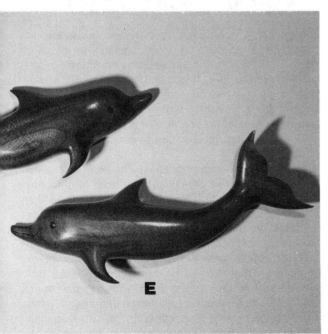

WILLIAM J. TADE

the longer the job will take. Machine burnishing can be done by mounting a smooth dowel in a power drill and carefully working the spinning dowel over the surface. This is tricky, but it can be done effectively. If lathe work has been involved in making the carving, you may return the piece to the lathe and simply press a bit of hardwood against the smoothed surface as it turns.

Wire-brushing is more a texturing method than a true finish. Use a wire brush, working with the grain, to abrade out the softer spring wood from between the layers of harder summer wood. This results in a highly textured surface, accentuating the natural grain pattern of the wood. The brushing may be done by hand, or a wire wheel may be mounted in a drill to speed up the process.

Sandblasting produces almost the same effects as wire-brushing by the use of air-blown particles of abrasive. Most large painting contractors and industrial painters can do this for you. It often leaves a slightly more pitted effect in the soft spring wood areas.

Charred-and-brushed finishes are produced by burning the surface with the flame of a gasoline, alcohol, propane, or acetylene torch, then removing the burned material with a wire brush. The surface should be burnt just enough so that red-hot, glowing lines appear under the flame but not enough so that the wood continues to burn when the torch is removed. A lightly dampened rag is good for squelching any flames that remain. The end effect is texturally similar to straight wire-brushing. Depth of color is controlled by severity of brushing. A light brushing, just enough to remove loose charred wood, leaves an alternately dull and shiny streaked black. Medium brushing leaves the hard summer wood a shiny black and the softer, more charred areas a deep chocolate to reddish-brown. Hard brushing lightens the black

BURNISH SURFACE by rubbing with chisel or other tool handle; wood will develop polished, glossy highlights.

WIRE-BRUSHED SURFACE (at right) has definite grain texture; brushing is done by hand or wire wheel.

to gray-brown, the brown approaching the original color of the wood. Fir, pine, and redwoods with prominent spring/summer wood patterns are especially spectacular with this finish.

EASY FINISHES

Petroleum jelly may be used as a simple but effective finish that gives a silky feel and appearance. It does not leave a sticky residue, as you might expect. Shoe polish is widely used as a coloring agent and finish for carvings. The liquid shoe polishes tend to produce deeper colors, since they soak into the wood. The solid wax-type polishes are easiest to use where uniform coloration is desired.

Food containers and utensils require non-poisonous finishes. Beeswax may be melted, thinned with mineral oil, and applied hot. Carved kitchen utensils should be periodically rubbed down with olive or salad oil to keep the wood from drying out or becoming water-soaked. Unfortunately, neither beeswax nor salad oil provide adequate protection against detergents, heat, or solvents. For bowls that will be exposed to strongly alkaline or acid foods, use a varnish, lacquer, or penetrating finish specifically labeled for use on wooden food-containers. These preparations are readily available from mail-order houses catering to the woodcraft hobbyist.

Whatever the finish, carved kitchen utensils should be periodically rubbed down with olive or salad oil to keep the wood from drying out or becoming waterlogged. Wash and dry as fast as possible to help prevent swelling, cracking, and finish damage.

STANDARD WOOD FINISHES

The finishing techniques described in the following pages are presented in their simplest forms. For more detail refer to the *Sunset* book *Furniture Finishing and Refinishing.* If you anticipate special problems, such as selecting paints for outdoor signs or ornaments, it is wise to write directly to the various manufacturers. Your local dealer may sometimes lack sufficient product information to cover your specialized needs.

Tool-marked areas should be checked to ensure that all surfaces are crisply cut. Surfaces to be made tool-mark free should be scraped or sanded to the desired smoothness. Remember that any rough spots or raised fiber will look crude and dark under the protective finish.

Water stains raise wood grain and should *never* be used on tool-marked or burnished surfaces. But with careful surface preparation, you may use them advantageously on other carvings. If you intend using water stains or any other material that will raise the grain, first sponge the surface with just enough warm water to color the wood but not enough to drench it or leave a water film. Let dry overnight, then sand off raised grain. Some woods, especially the softer ones, tend to develop a fine fuzz when sanded. To remove fuzz, apply a wash coat of shellac sizing-sealer (1 part 4-pound cut shellac to 4 parts denatured alcohol, brushed on as a single thin coat), a commercial sanding sealer, or a non-sealing glue size. Then dry thoroughly and fine-sand to remove the stiffened fibers.

Fillers. Except for pieces intended to be painted, woodcarvers seldom use fillers, since the wood texture is usually considered an integral part of a carving.

If you decide to use a filler, select a high-quality silex paste filler to go under clear finishes. The label should list silex, and the product should resemble a cream-colored peanut butter. Thin, using the recommended thinner (usually turpentine), to a thick house-paint or whipping cream consistency before applying. Color may be added by mixing in universal color pigments. Always use a thin wash-coat of shellac (1 part of 4-pound cut shellac to 8 parts denatured alcohol), or a compatible commercial sanding-sealer *under* the filler to prevent muddying, staining, or possible bleeding of stain into the filler.

Carvings to be painted may be prepared with silex filler, plasterer's spackle, or artist's gesso if all wood and tool-mark character is to be obliterated.

Coloring with stains and bleaches. Any stain or paint product may be used to color carvings—subject to certain precautions.

Water stains designed for wood are reasonably permanent but, as noted above, should not be used on tool-marked or burnished pieces. Fabric dyes offer interesting colors but are less long-lasting.

Bleaches are water-based, and should be used only within the limitations listed for water stains. Available bleaches include standard, full-strength, chlorinated laundry bleach, a saturated solution of oxalic acid which must be neutralized by a strong solution of borax after bleaching, and two-solution, industrial-strength, hydrogen peroxide bleaches, which can be dangerous if mishandled.

Alcohol stains and non-grain-raising (NGR) stains are fast drying, but are tricky to use because they tend to concentrate in any end-grain or soft spots, leaving a blotchy appearance.

Oil stains, consisting of dyes dissolved in oils, are easier to use than alcohol stains, but tend to be less permanent and somewhat hard to find in small quantities.

Sealer stains are essentially sealers, lacquer, or varnish mixed with dyes and pigments in suitable thinners. These are often available in spray cans and are easy to use after a little practice.

CHARRED FINISH is produced with clean torch flame. Use wire brush to remove loose, burned material.

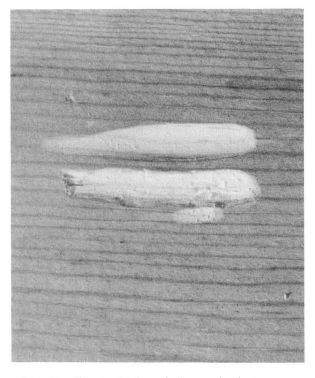

TOOL MARKS should be crisply cut (top); rough cut (bottom) will look crude and dark under protective finish.

Pigmented wiping stains are really diluted paint products. Most paints can be used as wiping stains— mix thoroughly, wipe on, allow to dry to a dull surface, then wipe down to remove excess pigments. But the vinyl latex wiping stains are particularly easy to handle and are available as pastes, foams, and in "dauber" bottles.

Padding stains and glazes are applied over the final finish for local tinting, touchup, or creating an antique-like effect.

Stain penetration into soft spring wood or end-grain can be controlled by pre-sealing the surfaces with thinned shellac or commercial sealer.

Clear finishes. Before applying *any* clear finish, use a tack rag (commercially available) to remove dust and minimize blemishes.

Wax. Hard carnauba floor wax is recommended. A gentle heating of both surface and wax will speed penetration of first coat. Allow to dry for an hour, then buff with fiber brush. Repeat as desired, and polish.

Oil. In a double boiler, heat equal parts boiled linseed oil and turpentine to 80°F. (WARNING: this is *very* flammable). Apply, and allow to soak in. Wipe free of oil. Then reapply—several times the first day, wiping dry each time. Apply once daily for a week, then once weekly for a month, and once monthly for a year to achieve maximum color and durability. Remember to dry and polish after each application.

Varnish-oil. Mix equal parts boiled linseed oil, turpentine, and top-quality spar varnish. Warm to 70°F. or above, then apply liberally with lint-free cloth. Let soak in, and rub vigorously until surface will absorb no more. Wring cloth dry and continue rubbing to remove all signs of wetness. Let dry for a week before reapplication or waxing.

Penetrating resin. Probably the simplest protective finish to apply. Depending on the specific wood, some darkening will occur. Apply resin and keep surfaces wet for a half-hour. Wipe off excess and polish with a clean, lint-free rag until all surface traces are removed. For maximum surface hardening and best color, repeat at 24-hour intervals until no more resin is absorbed. Remove any hardened surface residue by gently rubbing with 2/0 steel wool moistened in liquid resin.

Shellac. A fast, beautiful finishing agent, but sensitive to moisture, solvents, and rough handling. Purchase shellac fresh in one-time-use quantities. Old shellac goes bad on the shelf and leaves a non-drying, tacky surface. Use several coats of 1-pound cut shellac. It is far more forgiving of mistakes than single coats of 3 or 4-pound cut shellac. Though shellac is usually sold in either 3 or 4-pound cut consistencies, you can make your own 1-pound cut

by mixing 4 parts alcohol with 3 parts of 3-pound cut shellac, or 3 parts alcohol with 1 part of 4-pound cut shellac.

French polish. This is a tricky process involving multiple thin layers of shellac, applied by continuous rubbing with a lint-free pad soaked in ¾ or 1-pound cut shellac and lubricated with a drop or two of raw linseed oil. This method is often used with lathe turnings; the rubbing is then less tedious. Commercial synthetic French polishes are available from woodcraft mail order houses. They approximate the deep luster of true French polish and are a great deal easier to apply.

Lacquer is a fast-drying, synthetic finish available in both brushing and spraying formulas. Use the thinner recommended by the particular lacquer manufacturer. Mixing brands can lead to blemishes because of formula differences. Brushing-type floor lacquers are among the more widely available, and work well for carved furniture and carvings. Spray-can lacquers are excellent for most small carvings— just remember to remove the nozzles and clean them in lacquer thinner between uses. Lacquers will bleed many stains and pigments, and actually bleed natural colors from woods, unless the wood is shielded from them by lacquer sanding-sealer. Special bleed-resistant stains and fillers are available from lacquer manufacturers.

Varnishes. Where abrasion, weather, and resistance to abuse are prime considerations, varnishes provide full-bodied, tough finishes. However, varnish finishes that would be beautiful on furniture tend to look plastic on carvings; even without fillers, delicate wood textures can soften or vanish completely under an obviously thick finish. Dust is a special problem with varnishes, which remain tacky for relatively long periods. A good synthetic varnish is, in most cases, preferable to natural resin varnishes. Spar varnish should be avoided except for use on non-body contact carvings intended for exposure to weather or marine conditions.

Paints and glazes are used primarily for religious, commercial, insignia, and character carvings. The colors and contrasts offered provide high visibility and immediate recognition.

Paint and enamel products may be used as intended by the manufacturers, or as tints and glazes if first slightly thinned. Unthinned flat or semi-gloss paints may be used for whittled figures and other carvings; glossy enamels are the choice where intense color is more important than texture.

Thinned paints and enamels may be used as wiping stains, or applied as glazes over other finishes in the same way as products specifically designed as glazes.

Glazes are simply color pigments in a sealer or

varnish vehicle. A simple vehicle can be made by combining 8 parts satin varnish, 2 parts boiled linseed oil, and 1 part turpentine. Then add universal pigments to produce the color desired. Brush or pad glaze on base finish, then selectively remove with dry pad or brush to obtain the desired aged or highlighted effect. If the base finish coat itself has a varnish base, work fast so that the glaze vehicle will not penetrate the base coat. Latex-enamel base coats are excellent for glazing since they are relatively impervious to varnish-based glazes (in case of error, the glaze can be wiped off with turpentine without affecting the latex base).

Gilding. A high proportion of classic royal and religious carvings are gilded. While seldom used in modern carving, gilding still has a useful function as a means of high-lighting or providing contrasts to natural wood tones. Gilt is available in colors ranging from silver through pinks, golds, deep bronzes, and even bright colors.

The simplest application is by means of cosmetic-like *compos* (gilding powders in wax or varnish paste formulations) which are simply applied like shoe polish and buffed.

Bronzing is the process of spreading a bronzing liquid (high quality varnish or slow drying lacquer) to the appropriate area, allowing it to become tacky, then applying the gilding powder by brushing, dabbing, or blowing.

Leaf gilding involves the application of a rabbit-skin glue size, gilder's varnish size, or gilder's lacquer size to the surface. Allow the size to become tacky, then apply the leaf and carefully smooth it flat with a cotton ball. Patch gaps immediately with scrap leaf. Allow to dry at least 8 hours, then burnish with a piece of polished agate (obtainable from rock shops) or a velvet pad. Genuine gold leaf looks best when unprotected by a finish, but if the piece is to be handled, protect the leaf with a clear shellac or lacquer.

TO SAND OR NOT

Style will dictate how much finish sanding you do. Many styles of whittled, folk, and contemporary carvings depend on crisp tool-marks for texture and overall effect. But many examples of classical and modern sculpture, as well as countless decorative pieces, are finished to a glossy sheen with all tool marks sanded off. In between are dozens of styles, textures, and effects where you will have to be your own judge of the relative values of tool-marks versus sanding. Any group of carvers includes some who deride tool-marks as slovenly and others who condemn sanded surfaces as characterless. Listen to both, then follow your own taste.

There are several homemade sanding devices which can save you a lot of time and effort.

Flat, tapered, round, or oval sticks wrapped with abrasive cloth or paper are basic and easily made. The abrasive can be wrapped directly onto the sticks or over thin ⅛-inch layers of sponge rubber, inner tube, or felt pads.

A hand strip-sander is very useful. This simple gadget has a hacksaw-like frame which holds an abrasive strip, either slack or taut as desired. Strips

of various widths can be used to suit the work at hand.

Specially-contoured abrasive tools can be made. After shaping a piece of wood, plastic, or metal, apply glue and allow to dry until it starts to get tacky; then sprinkle abrasive grit onto the surface or roll the tacky-glued surface in loose grit. Permit the glue to dry thoroughly before using the tool. Using this technique, specially-shaped riffler substitutes can be made. Thread, string, or rope can be abrasive-coated for use with the strip-sander frame.

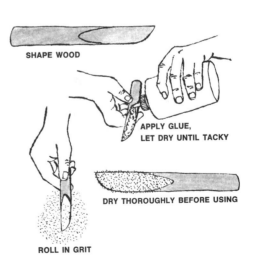

SHAPE WOOD

APPLY GLUE, LET DRY UNTIL TACKY

DRY THOROUGHLY BEFORE USING

ROLL IN GRIT

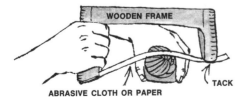

WOODEN FRAME

ABRASIVE CLOTH OR PAPER

TACK

Some Common Woodcarving Terms

BOSTING. The rough shaping of actual design elements.

BURL. A growth sometimes found on trees. The wood of a burl often has wildly beautiful grain patterns, but is hard to carve.

CALIPER. A hinged, two-legged instrument similar to a draftsman's compass. It is used for making and transferring measurements.

CHECK. A crack or split, either in a log or in cut lumber.

CHISEL. A tool having a single-beveled cutting edge at one end and used for shaping wood; driven either by hand or by tapping with a mallet.

CHUCK. A device for holding a cutting bit in a drill, grinder, lathe, or similar machine.

COLLET. A type of chuck having a compressible collar for holding cutting bits of like diameter.

DIAPER. A pattern produced by repetitive use of a simple design.

FIRMER. In carving, a flat-bladed, double-beveled chisel.

FITCH. A thin sheet of wood used as veneer or as a layer in plywood.

GESSO. A smooth, pliable, plaster-like workable mixture used to provide a smooth surface. for painting or gilding.

GRINDER. A machine with rotating abrasive wheels for sharpening tools. Also an electric tool used with burrs and bits for shaping wood.

GROUND. The background area of a surface carving.

HEARTWOOD. The hard portion of a tree trunk close to the center.

KERF. The path cut through wood by a saw blade.

LEADING. A white lead-based glaze. Also, the process of adding lead to the bases of top-heavy carvings.

MODEL. To carve or shape to final contours.

QUICK GOUGE. Any gouge with a small radius cutting edge.

ROUGH OUT. To make broad, undetailed rough cuts.

SAPWOOD. The softer, usually lighter, colored wood between bark and heartwood of a tree.

SEMI-FIRMER. A single-beveled, flat-bladed chisel with a slight roll-off on bevel on the normally flat side.

SET IN. To outline a design with stop-cuts prior to removing unwanted wood.

SKEW. A firmer having its cutting edge set at an angle to the tool axis.

SPRINGWOOD. The softer wood layers in the tree ring-pattern, grown during spring or wet weather.

STOP CUTS. To cut vertically into a surface, to outline and provide protection against accidental splitting while removing excess wood.

STRIKE. To make stop-cuts in chip carving.

STUMP. The ground level and root portion of a tree; sometimes containing grain patterns.

SUMMERWOOD. The harder wood layers in the tree ring-pattern, grown during summer or dry seasons.

TANG. The spike-like extension of a chisel blade that fits into the wooden handle.

UNDERCUT. To cut back beneath an exposed edge.

PHOTOGRAPHS by James B. Johnstone except the following: Ells Marugg: pages 30 (top right), 43 (right). Don Normark: pages 31, 35 (top), 47 (bottom right). Alyson Smith: pages 56 (bottom right), 75.